TALES FROM ERIN

AN ANTHOLOGY OF RARE IRISH LEGENDS

BOOK ONE

Edited by

Lizzy Shannon

Sheffield Publications

TALES FROM ERIN

AN ANTHOLOGY OF RARE IRISH LEGENDS

BOOK ONE

Edited by

Lizzy Shannon

Sheffield Publications

Sheffield Publications

10 9 8 7 6 5 4 3 2

Tales from Erin – Book One

ISBN-13: 978-0692255407 (Sheffield Publications)
ISBN-10: 0692255400

The text for this book was set in Cambria.

Printed and bound in the United States of America.

For Grilka

"True friends are always together in spirit."
L.M. Montgomery

CONTENTS

1.

THE THREE DAUGHTERS
OF KING O'HARA

THERE WAS a king in Desmond whose name was Coluath O'Hara, and he had three daughters. On a time when he was away from home, the eldest daughter took a thought that she'd like to be married. So she went up in the castle, put on the cloak of darkness that her father had, and wished for the most beautiful man under the sun as a husband for herself. She got her wish, for scarcely had she put off the cloak of darkness when there came, in a golden coach with four horses, two black and two white, the finest man she had ever laid eyes on, and he took her away.

When the second daughter saw what had happened to her sister, she put on the cloak of darkness, and wished for the next best man in the world as a husband. She put off the cloak; and straightway there came, in a golden coach with four black horses, a man nearly as good as the first, and took her away.

The third sister put on the cloak, and wished for the best white dog in the world. Presently he came, with one man attending, in a golden coach and four snow-white horses, and took the youngest sister away.

When the king came home, the stable-boy told him what had happened while he was gone. He was enraged beyond measure when he heard that his youngest daughter had wished for a white dog, and gone off with him.

When the first man brought his wife home he asked, "In what form will you have me in the daytime; as I am now or as I am at night?"

"As you are now in the daytime."

So the first sister had her husband as a man during the day, but at night he was a seal.

The second man put the same question to the middle sister and got the same answer, so she had her husband in the same form as the first.

When the third sister came to where the white dog lived, he asked her, "How will you have me to be in the daytime; as I am now, or as I am at night?"

"As you are now in the day."

So the white dog was a dog in the daytime, but the most beautiful of men at night.

After a time the third sister had a son. One day, when the child was a week old, her husband went out to hunt, and warned her that if anything should happen to the child, not to shed a tear on that account. While he was gone, a great gray crow that used to haunt the place came and carried the child away. Remembering the warning, she shed not a tear for the loss.

All went on as before till another son was born. The husband went hunting every day, and again he said she must not shed a tear if anything happened. When the child was a week old a great gray crow came and bore him away; but the mother did not cry or drop a tear.

All went well till a daughter was born. When she was a week old a great gray crow came and swept her away. This time the mother dropped one tear on a handkerchief, which she took out of her pocket, and then put back again.

When the husband came home from hunting and heard what the crow had done, he asked the wife, "Have you shed tears this time?"

"I have dropped one tear," confessed she.

He was very angry; for he knew what harm she had done by dropping that one tear.

Soon after their father invited the three sisters to visit him and be present at a great feast in their honor. They sent messages, each from her own place that they would attend.

The king was very glad at the prospect of seeing his children. But the queen was grieved, and thought it a great disgrace that her youngest daughter had no one to come home with her but a white dog.

The white dog was in dread that the king wouldn't let him inside with the company, but would drive him from the castle to the yard. And that the dogs outside wouldn't leave a patch of skin on his back, but would tear the life out of him.

The youngest daughter comforted him. "There is no danger to you," said she, "for wherever I am, you'll be, and wherever you go, I'll follow and take care of you."

When all was ready for the feast at the castle, and all were assembled, the king was for banishing the white dog; but the youngest daughter would not listen to her father. She would not let the white dog out of her sight, but kept him near her at the feast, and divided with him the food that came to herself.

When the feast was over, and all the guests had gone, the three sisters went to their own rooms in the castle.

Late in the evening the queen took the cook with her, and while all three were asleep she stole in to see what was in her daughters' rooms. What should she see by the side of her youngest daughter but the most beautiful man she had ever laid eyes on.

Then she went to where the other two daughters slept. There, instead of the two men who brought them to the feast, were two seals, fast asleep. The queen was greatly troubled at the sight of the seals. When she and the cook were returning, they came upon the skin of the white dog. She caught it up as she went, and threw it into the kitchen fire.

The skin was not five minutes in the fire when it gave a crack that woke not only all in the castle, but all in the country for miles around.

The husband of the youngest daughter sprang up. He was very angry and very sorry. "If I had been able to spend three nights with you under your father's roof," he said, "I should have got back my own form again for good, and could have been a man both in the day and the night; but now I must go."

He rose from the bed and ran out of the castle. Away he went as fast as ever his two legs could carry him, overtaking the one before him, and leaving the one behind. He was this way all that night and the next day; but he couldn't leave the wife, for she followed from the castle, was after him in the night and the day too, and never lost sight of him.

In the afternoon he turned, and told her to go back to her father, but she would not listen to him. At nightfall they came to the first house they had seen since leaving the castle. He turned and said, "Do you go inside and stay in this house till morning. I'll pass the night outside where I am."

The wife went in. The woman of the house rose up, gave her a pleasant welcome, and put a good supper before her. She was not long in the house when a little boy came to her knee and called her, "Mother."

The woman of the house told the child to go back to his place, and not to come out again.

"Here are a pair of scissors," said the woman of the house to the king's daughter. "They will serve you well. Whatever ragged people you see, if you cut a piece off their rags, that moment they will have new clothes of gold cloth."

The daughter stayed that night, for she had good welcome. Next morning when she went out, her husband said, "You'd better go home now to your father."

"I'll not go to my father if I have to leave you," said she.

So he went on, and she followed. It was that way all the day till night came. At nightfall they saw another house at the foot of a hill, and again the husband stopped and said, "You go in; I'll stop outside till morning."

The woman of the house gave her a good welcome. After she had eaten and drunk, a little boy came out of another room, ran to her knee, and said, "Mother." The woman of the house sent the boy back to where he had come from, and told him to stay there.

Next morning, when the princess was going out to her husband, the woman of the house gave her a comb, and said, "If you meet any person with a diseased and a sore head, and draw this comb over it three times, the head will be well, and covered with the most beautiful golden hair ever seen."

She took the comb, and went out to her husband.

"Leave me now," said he, "and go back to your father."

"I will not," said she. "I will follow you while I have the power." So they went forward that day, as on the other two.

At nightfall they came to a third house at the foot of a hill, where the princess received a good welcome. After she had eaten supper, a little girl with only one eye came to her knee and said, "Mother."

The princess began to cry at sight of the child, thinking that she herself was the cause that it had but one eye. She put her hand into her pocket where she kept the handkerchief on which she had dropped the tear when the gray crow carried her infant away. She had never used it since that day, for there was an eye on it.

She opened the handkerchief, and put the eye in the girl's head. It grew into the socket that minute, and the child saw out of it as well as out of the other eye. Then the woman of the house sent the little one to bed.

Next morning, as the king's daughter was going out, the woman of the house gave her a whistle, and said, "Whenever you put this whistle to your mouth and blow on it, all the birds of the air will come to you from every quarter under the sun. Take care of the whistle, as it may serve you greatly."

"Go back to your father's castle," said the husband when she came to him, "for I must leave you today." They went on together a few hundred yards, and then sat on a green hillock. "Your mother has come between us," he told his wife. "But for her we might have lived together all our days. If I had been allowed to pass three nights with you in your father's house, I should have got back my form of a man both in the daytime and the night. The Queen of *Tir na n-Og*, the land of youth, enchanted and put on me a spell. Unless I could spend three nights with a wife under her father's roof in Erin, I should bear the form of a white dog one half of my time. But if the skin of the dog should be burned before the three nights were over, I must go down to her kingdom and marry the queen herself. And it is to her I am going today. I have no power to stay, and I must leave you. So farewell, you'll never see me again on the upper earth."

He left her crying on the mound, went a few steps forward to some bulrushes, pulled up one, and disappeared in the opening where the rush had been.

His wife stayed there, sitting on the mound lamenting, till evening, not knowing what to do. At last she bethought herself, and going to the rushes, pulled up a stalk, went down, followed her husband, and never stopped till she came to the lower land.

After a while she reached a small house near a splendid castle. She went into the house and asked, could she stay there till morning.

"You can," said the woman of the house, "and welcome."

Next day the woman was washing clothes, for that was how she made a living. The princess fell to and helped her with the work. In the course of that day the Queen of *Tir na n-Og* and the husband of the princess were married.

Near the castle, and not far from the washerwoman's lived a henwife with two ragged little daughters. One of them came around the washerwoman's house to play. The child looked so poor and her clothes were so torn and dirty that the princess took pity on her, and cut the clothes with the scissors that she had been given. That moment the most beautiful dress of gold cloth ever seen on woman or child in that kingdom was on the henwife's daughter.

When she saw what she had on, the child ran home to her mother as fast as ever she could go.

"Who gave you that dress?" asked the henwife.

"A strange woman that is in that house beyond," said the little girl, pointing to the washerwoman's home.

The henwife went straight to the Queen of *Tir na n-Og* and said, "There is a strange woman in the place, who will be likely to take your husband from you, unless you banish her away or do something to her. For she has a pair of scissors different from anything ever seen or heard of in this country."

When the queen heard this she sent word to the princess that unless the scissors were given up to her without delay, she would have the head off her. The princess said she would give up the scissors if the queen would let her spend one night with her husband. The queen answered that she was willing to give her the one night. The princess came and gave up the scissors, and went to her own husband. But the queen had given him a drink and he fell asleep, and never woke till after the princess had gone in the morning. Next day another daughter of the henwife went to the washerwoman's house to play. She was wretched looking, her head being covered with scabs and sores. The princess drew the comb three times over the child's head, cured it, and covered it with beautiful golden hair. The little girl ran home and told her mother how the strange woman had healed her.

The henwife hurried off to the queen. "That strange woman has a comb with wonderful power to cure and give golden hair. She'll take your husband from you unless you banish her or take her life."

The queen sent word to the princess that unless she gave up the comb, she would have her life. The princess returned as answer that she would give up the comb if she might pass one night with the queen's husband. The queen was willing, and gave her husband a draught as before. When the princess came, he was fast asleep, and did not waken till after she had gone in the morning.

On the third day the washerwoman and the princess went out to walk, and the first daughter of the henwife with them. When they were outside the town, the princess put the whistle to her mouth and blew. That moment the birds of the air flew to her from every direction in flocks. Among them was a bird of song and new tales.

The princess went to one side with the bird. "What means can I take," asked she, "against the queen to get back my husband? Is it best to kill her, and can I do it?"

"It is very hard," answered the bird, "to kill her. There is no one in all *Tir na n-Og* who is able to take her life but her own husband. Inside a holly-tree in front of the castle is a *wether*. In the *wether* a duck, in the duck an egg, and in that egg is her heart and life. No man in *Tir na n-Og* can cut that holly tree but her husband.''

The princess blew the whistle again. A fox and a hawk came to her. She caught and put them into two boxes, which the washerwoman had with her, and took them to her new home.

When the henwife's daughter went home, she told her mother about the whistle. Away ran the henwife to the queen. ''That strange woman has a whistle that brings together all the birds of the air, and she'll have your husband yet, unless you take her head.''

''I'll take the whistle from her, anyhow,'' said the queen. So she sent for the whistle.

The princess gave answer that she would give up the whistle if she might pass one night with the queen's husband. The queen agreed, and gave him a draught as on the other nights. He was asleep when the princess came and when she went away. Before going, the princess left a letter with his servant for the queen's husband, in which she told how she had followed him to *Tir na n-Og*, and had given the scissors, the comb, and the whistle, to pass three nights in his company, but had not spoken to him because the queen had given him sleeping draughts. She told him that the life of the queen was in an egg, the egg in a duck, the duck in a *wether*, the *wether* in a holly-tree in front of the castle, and that no man could split the tree but himself.

As soon as he got the letter the husband took an axe and went to the holly-tree. He found the princess there before him, having the two boxes with the fox and the hawk in them. He struck the tree a few blows; it split open, and out sprang the *wether*. He ran scarce twenty perches before the fox caught him. The fox tore him open; then the duck flew out. The duck had not flown fifteen perches when the hawk caught and killed her, smashing the egg. That instant the Queen of *Tir na n-Og* died.

The husband kissed and embraced his faithful wife. He gave a great feast, and when it was over, he burned the henwife with her house, built a palace for the washerwoman, and made his servant secretary. They never left *Tir na n-Og*, and are living there happily now; and so may we live here.

2.

THE WEAVER'S DON AND THE GIANT OF THE WHITE HILL

THERE WAS once a weaver in Erin who lived at the edge of a wood. On a time when he had nothing to burn, he went out with his daughter to get fagots for the fire.

They gathered two bundles, and were ready to carry them home, when who should come along but a splendid-looking stranger on horseback. He said to the weaver, "My good man, will you give me that girl of yours?"

"Indeed then I will not," replied the weaver.

"I'll give you her weight in gold," said the stranger, and he put out the gold there on the ground.

So the weaver went home with the gold and without the daughter. He buried the gold in the garden, without letting his wife know what he had done. When she asked, "Where is our daughter?" he said. "I sent her on an errand to a neighbor's house for things that I want."

Night came, but no sight of the girl. The next time he went for fagots, the weaver took his second daughter to the wood. When they had two bundles gathered and were ready to go home, a second stranger came on horseback, much finer than the first, and asked the weaver would he give him his daughter.

"I will not," said the weaver.

"Well," said the stranger, "I'll give you her weight in silver if you let her go with me." He put the silver down before him.

The weaver carried home the silver and buried it in the garden with the gold, and the daughter went away with the man on horseback. When he went again to the wood, the weaver took his third daughter with him. When they were ready to go home, a third man came on horseback, gave the weight of the third daughter in copper, and took her away. The weaver buried the copper with the gold and silver.

Now, the wife lamented and moaned night and day for her three daughters, and gave the weaver no rest till he told the whole story.

Now, a son was born to them, and when the boy grew up and went to school, he heard how his three sisters had been carried away for their weight in gold and silver and copper. Every day he came home he saw how his mother was lamenting and wandering outside in grief through the fields and pits and ditches. He asked her what trouble was on her, but she wouldn't tell him a word.

At last one day he came home crying from school, and said, "I'll not sleep three nights in one house till I find my three sisters." Then he said to his mother, "Make me three loaves of bread, Mother, for I am going on a journey." Next day he asked had she the bread ready. She said she had, and cried bitterly. "I'm going to leave you now, Mother," said he. "I'll come back when I have found my three sisters."

He went away, and walked on till he was tired and hungry. When he sat down to eat the bread that his mother had given him, a red-haired man came up and asked him for something to eat. "Sit down here," said the boy. He sat, and the two ate till there was not a crumb of the bread left.

The boy told of the journey he was on, and the red-haired man said, "There may not be much use in your going, but here are three things that'll serve you. The sword of sharpness, the cloth of plenty, and the cloak of darkness. No man can kill you while that sword is in your hand. Whenever you are hungry or dry, all you have to do is to spread the cloth and ask for what you'd like to eat or drink, and it will be there before you. When you put on the cloak, there won't be a man or a woman or a living thing in the world that'll see you, and you'll go to whatever place you have set your mind on quicker than any wind."

The red-haired man went his way, and the boy traveled on. Before evening a great shower came, and he ran for shelter to a large oak tree. When he got near the tree his foot slipped, the ground opened, and down he went through the earth till he came to another country. He put on the cloak of darkness and went ahead like a blast of wind, and never stopped till he saw a castle in the distance, and soon he was there. But he found nine gates closed before him, and no way to go through. It was written inside the cloak of darkness that his eldest sister lived in that castle.

He was not long at the gate looking in when a girl came to him. "Go on out of that," she warned. "If you don't, you'll be killed."

"Do you go in," said he to the girl, "and tell my sister, the woman of this castle, to come out to me."

The girl ran in, out came the sister, and asked, "Why are you here, and what did you come for?"

"I have come to this country to find my three sisters, who were given away by my father for their weight in gold, silver, and copper. You are my eldest sister."

She knew from what he said that he was her brother, so she opened the gates and brought him in. "Don't wonder at anything you see in this castle. My husband is enchanted. I see him only at night. He goes off every morning, stays away all day, and comes home in the evening." The sun went down; and while they were talking, the husband rushed in, and the noise of him was terrible. He came in the form of a ram, ran upstairs, and soon after came down a man.

"Who is this that's with you?" asked he of the wife.

"Oh, that's my brother, who has come from Erin to see me," said she.

Next morning, when the man of the castle was going off in the form of a ram, he turned to the boy. "Will you stay a few days in my castle? You are welcome."

"Nothing would please me better," said the boy. "But I have made a vow never to sleep three nights in one house till I have found my three sisters."

"Well," said the ram. "Since you must go, here is something for you." He pulled out a bit of his own wool and gave it to the boy. "Keep this. Whenever a trouble is on you, take it out, and call on what rams are in the world to help you."

Away went the ram. The boy took farewell of his sister, put on the cloak of darkness, and disappeared. He traveled till hungry and tired, then sat down, took off the cloak of darkness, spread the cloth of plenty, and asked for meat and drink. After he had eaten and drunk his fill, he took up the cloth, put on the cloak of darkness, and went ahead, bypassing every wind that was before him, and leaving every wind that was behind.

About an hour before sunset he saw the castle in which his second sister lived. When he reached the gate, a girl came out to him and said, "Go away from that gate, or you'll be killed."

"I'll not leave this till my sister who lives in the castle comes out and speaks to me."

The girl ran in, and out came the sister. When she heard

his story and his father's name, she knew that he was her brother. "Come into the castle, but think nothing of what you'll see or hear. I don't see my husband from morning till night. He goes and comes in a strange form, but he is a man at night."

About sunset there was a terrible noise, and in rushed the man of the castle in the form of a tremendous salmon. He went flapping upstairs, but he wasn't long there till he came down a fine-looking man. "Who is that with you?" asked he of the wife. "I thought you would let no one into the castle while I was gone."

"Oh, this is my brother, who has come to see me," said she.

"If he's your brother, he's welcome," said the man.

They supped, and then slept till morning. When the man of the castle was going out again in the form of a great salmon, he turned to the boy. "You'd better stay here with us a while."

"I cannot," said the boy. "I made a vow never to sleep three nights in one house till I had seen my three sisters. I must go on now and find my third sister."

The salmon then took off a piece of his fin and gave it to the boy. "If any difficulty meets you, or trouble comes on you, call on what salmons are in the sea to come and help you."

They parted. The boy put on his cloak of darkness, and away he went, more swiftly than any wind. He never stopped till he was hungry and thirsty. Then he sat down, took off his cloak of darkness, spread the cloth of plenty, and ate his fill. When he had eaten, he went on again till near sundown, until he saw the castle where his third sister lived. All three castles were near the sea. Neither sister knew what place she was in, and neither knew where the other two were living.

The third sister took her brother in just as the first and

second had done, telling him not to wonder at anything he saw. They were not long inside when a roaring noise was heard, and in came the greatest eagle that ever was seen. The eagle hurried upstairs, and soon came down a man. "Who is that stranger there with you?" asked he of the wife. He, as well as the ram and salmon, knew the boy; he only wanted to test his wife.

"This is my brother, who has come to see me."

They all took supper and slept that night. When the eagle was going away in the morning, he pulled a feather out of his wing, and said to the boy, "Keep this; it may serve you. If you are ever in straits and want help, call on what eagles are in the world, and they'll come to you."

There was no hurry now, for the third sister was found. The boy went upstairs with her to examine the country all around, and to look at the sea. Soon he saw a great white hill, and on the top of the hill a castle.

"In that castle on the white hill beyond," said the sister, "lives a giant, who stole from her home the most beautiful young woman in the world. From all parts the greatest heroes and champions and kings' sons are coming to take her away from the giant and marry her. There is not a man of them all who is able to conquer the giant and free the young woman. The giant conquers them, cuts their heads off, and then eats their flesh. When he has picked the bones clean, he throws them out. The whole place around the castle is white with the bones of the men that the giant has eaten."

"I must go," said the boy, "to that castle to know can I kill the giant and bring away the young woman."

So he took leave of his sister, put on the cloak of darkness, took his sword with him, and was soon inside the castle. The giant was fighting with champions outside. When the boy saw the young woman he took off the cloak of darkness and spoke to her.

"Oh!" said she. "What can you do against the giant? No man has ever come to this castle without losing his life. The giant kills every man. No one has ever come here so big that the giant did not eat him at one meal."

"And is there no way to kill him?" asked the boy.

"I think not," said she.

"Well, if you'll give me something to eat, I'll stay here. When the giant comes in, I'll do my best to kill him. But don't let on that I am here."

Then he put on the cloak of darkness, and no one could see him. When the giant came in, he had the bodies of two men on his back. He threw them down and told the young woman to get them ready for his dinner. Then he snuffed around. "There's someone here; I smell the blood of an Erineach."

"I don't think you do," said the young woman. "I can't see anyone."

"Neither can I," said the giant. "But I smell a man."

With that the boy drew his sword. When the giant was struck, he ran in the direction of the blow to give one back, and then he was struck on the other side. They were at one another this way, the giant and the boy with the cloak of darkness on him, till the giant had fifty wounds, and was covered with blood. Every minute he was getting a slash of a sword, but never could give one back.

At last he called out, "Whoever you are, wait till tomorrow and I'll face you then."

So the fighting stopped. The young woman began to cry and lament as if her heart would break when she saw the state the giant was in. "Oh, you'll be with me no longer; you'll be killed now. What can I do alone without you?" She tried to please him, and washed his wounds.

"Don't be afraid," said the giant. "This one, whoever he is, will not kill me, for there is no man in the world that can kill me." Then he went to bed, and was well in the morning.

Next day the giant and the boy began in the middle of the forenoon, and fought till the middle of the afternoon. The giant was covered with wounds, but he had not given one blow to the boy. He could not see him, for he was always in his cloak of darkness. So the giant had to ask for rest till next morning.

While the young woman was washing and dressing the giant's wounds she cried and lamented all the time. "What'll become of me now? I'm afraid you'll be killed this time. How can I live here without you?"

"Have no fear for me," said the giant. "I'll put your mind at rest. In the bottom of the sea is a chest locked and bound. In that chest is a duck, in the duck an egg, and I never can be killed unless someone gets the egg from the duck in the chest at the bottom of the sea, and rubs it on the mole that is under my right arm."

While the giant told this to the woman, who should be listening to the story but the boy in the cloak of darkness. The minute he heard of the chest in the sea, he thought of the salmons. So off he hurried to the seashore, which was not far away. Then he took out the fin that his eldest sister's husband had given him, and called on what salmons were in the sea to bring up the chest with the duck inside, and put it out on the beach before him.

He had not long to wait till he saw nothing but salmon; the whole sea was covered with them, moving to land. They put the chest out on the beach before him. But the chest was locked and strong. The boy pulled out the ram's wool, and cried, "I want what rams are in the world to come and break open this chest!"

That minute the rams of the world were running to the seashore, each with a terrible pair of horns on him. Soon they battered the chest to splinters. Out flew the duck, and away she went over the sea.

The boy took out the feather. "I want what eagles are in the world to get me the egg from that duck."

That minute the duck was surrounded by the eagles of the world, and the egg was soon brought to the boy. He put the feather, the wool, and the fin in his pocket, put on the cloak of darkness, and went to the castle on the white hill. He told the young woman, as she dressed the wounds of the giant again, to raise up his arm.

Next day they fought till the middle of the afternoon. The giant was almost cut to pieces, and called for a cessation. The young woman hurried to dress the wounds, and he said, "I see you would help me if you could; you are not able. But never fear. I shall not be killed." Then she raised his arm to wash away the blood, and the boy, who was there in his cloak of darkness, struck the mole with the egg. The giant died that minute.

The boy took the young woman to the castle of his third sister. Next day he went back for the treasures of the giant, and there was more gold in the castle than one horse could draw. They spent nine days in the castle of the eagle with the third sister. Then the boy gave back the feather, and the two went on till they came to the castle of the salmon. There they spent nine more days with the second sister, and he gave back the fin. When they came to the castle of the ram, they spent fifteen days with the first sister, and had great feasting and enjoyment. Then the boy gave back the lock of wool to the ram, and took farewell of his sister and her husband. He set out for home with the young woman of the white castle, who was now his wife, bringing presents from the three daughters to their father and mother. At last they reached the opening near the tree, came up through the ground, and went on to where he met the red-haired man. Then he spread the cloth of plenty, asked for every good meat and drink, and called the red-haired man. He came. The three sat down, ate and drank with enjoyment. When they had finished, the boy gave back to the red-haired man the cloak of darkness, the sword of sharpness, and the cloth of plenty, and thanked him.

"You were kind to me," said the red-haired man. "You gave me of your bread when I asked for it, and told me where you were going. I took pity on you; for I knew you never could get what you wanted unless I helped you. I am the brother of the eagle, the salmon, and the ram."

They parted. The boy went home, built a castle with the treasure of the giant, and lived happily with his parents and wife.

3.

THE STOLEN BRIDE

ABOUT THE year 1670, there was a fine young fellow living at a place called Querin, in County Clare. He was brave and strong and rich, for he had his own land and his own house, and no one to lord it over him. He was called the Kern of Querin. And many a time he would go out alone to shoot the wild fowl at night along the lonely strand and sometimes cross over northward to the broad east strand, about two miles away, to find the wild geese.

One cold frosty November Eve he was watching for them, crouched down behind the ruins of an old hut, when a loud splashing noise attracted his attention. "It is the wild geese," he said to himself. Raising his gun, he waited in death-like silence for the approach of his prey.

But presently he saw a dark mass moving along the edge of the strand and knew there were no wild geese near him. So he watched and waited till the black mass came closer, and he distinctly perceived four stout men carrying a bier on their shoulders, on which lay a corpse covered with a white cloth. For a few moments they laid it down, apparently to rest themselves, and the Kern instantly fired. The four men ran away shrieking, and the corpse was left alone on the bier. Kern of Querin immediately sprang to the place, and lifting the cloth from the face of the corpse, beheld by the freezing starlight, the form of a beautiful young girl, apparently not dead but in a deep sleep.

Gently he passed his hand over her face and raised her up. When she opened her eyes she looked around with wild wonder, but spake never a word, though he tried to soothe and encourage her. Thinking it was dangerous for them to remain in that place, he raised her from the bier, and taking her hand led her away to his own house. They arrived safely, but in silence. And for twelve months did she remain with the Kern, never tasting food or speaking word for all that time.

When the next November Eve came round, he resolved to visit the east strand again. He'd watch from the same place, in the hope of meeting with some adventure that might throw light on the history of the beautiful girl. His way lay beside the old ruined fort called Lios-na-fallainge, the Fort of the Mantle, and as he passed, the sound of music and mirth fell on his ear.

He stopped to catch the words of the voices, and had not waited long when he heard a man say in a low whisper, "Where shall we go tonight to carry off a bride?"

And a second voice answered, "Wherever we go I hope better luck will be ours than we had this day twelvemonths."

"Yes," said a third. "On that night we carried off a rich prize, the fair daughter of O'Connor; but that clown, the Kern of Querin, broke our spell and took her from us. Yet little pleasure has he had of his bride, for she has neither eaten nor drank nor uttered a word since she entered his house."

"And so she will remain," said a fourth, "until he makes her eat off her father's tablecloth, which covered her as she lay on the bier, and which is now thrown up over the top of her bed."

On hearing all this, the Kern rushed home. Without waiting even for the morning, entered the young girl's room, took down the tablecloth, spread it on the table, laid meat and drink thereon, and led her to it. "Drink," he said, "that speech may come to you."

And she drank, and ate of the food, and then speech came. She told the Kern her story: how she was to have been married to a young lord of her own country. The wedding guests had all assembled when she felt herself suddenly ill and swooned away. She never knew more of what had happened to her until the Kern had passed his hand over her face, by which she recovered consciousness, but could neither eat nor speak, for a spell was on her, and she was helpless.

Then the Kern prepared a chariot, and carried home the young girl to her father, who was like to die for joy when he beheld her. And the Kern grew mightily in O'Connor's favor, so that at last he gave him his fair young daughter to wife. The wedded pair lived together happily for many long years after, and no evil befell them, but good followed all the work of their hands.

This story of Kern of Querin still lingers in the faithful, vivid Irish memory. It is often told by the peasants of Clare when they gather round the fire on the awful festival of Samhain, or November Eve, when the dead walk, and the spirits of earth and air have power over mortals, whether for good or evil.

4.

THE HORNED WOMEN

A RICH woman sat up late one night carding and preparing wool, while all the family and servants were asleep. Suddenly a knock was given at the door, and a voice called, "Open! Open!"

"Who is there?" asked the woman of the house.

"I am the Witch of one Horn," was answered.

The mistress, supposing that one of her neighbors had called and required assistance, opened the door. A woman entered, having in her hand a pair of wool-carders, and bearing a horn on her forehead, as if growing there. She sat down by the fire in silence, and began to card the wool with violent haste.

Then she paused, and said, "Where are the women? They delay too long."

A second knock came to the door, and a voice called as before, "Open! Open!"

The mistress felt herself obliged to rise and open the door, and immediately a second witch entered, having two horns on her forehead, and in her hand a wheel for spinning wool.

"Give me place," she said. "I am the Witch of the two Horns." She began to spin as quick as lightning.

And so the knocks went on, and the call was heard. The

witches entered, until at last twelve women sat round the fire; the first with one horn and the last with twelve horns. They carded the thread and turned their spinning-wheels, and wound and wove, all singing together an ancient rhyme, but no word did they speak to the mistress of the house.

Strange to hear, and frightful to look upon, were these twelve women, with their horns and their wheels. The mistress felt near to death, and she tried to rise that she might call for help. But she could not move, nor could she utter a word or a cry, for the spell of the witches was upon her.

Then one of them called to her in Irish. "Rise, woman, and make us a cake."

The mistress searched for a vessel to bring water from the well that she might mix the meal and make the cake, but she could find none.

They said to her, "Take a sieve and bring water in it."

She took the sieve and went to the well, but the water poured from it and she could fetch none for the cake. She sat down by the well and wept.

Then a voice came by her and said, "Take yellow clay and moss, and bind them together, and plaster the sieve so that it will hold."

This she did, and the sieve held the water for the cake. The voice spoke again. "Return, and when thou comest to the north angle of the house, cry aloud three times and say, '*The mountain of the Fenian women and the sky over it is all on fire.*'"

And she did so.

When the witches inside heard the call, a great and terrible cry broke from their lips. They rushed forth with wild lamentations and shrieks, and fled away to Slievenamon, where was their chief abode.

The Spirit of the Well bade the mistress of the house to enter and prepare her home against the enchantments of the witches if they returned again.

First, to break their spells, she sprinkled the water in which she had washed her child's feet, the feet-water, outside the door on the threshold.

Secondly, she took the cake, which in her absence the witches had made of meal mixed with the blood drawn from the sleeping family, and she broke it in bits. Placing a piece in the mouth of each sleeper, they were restored.

Then she took the cloth they had woven, and placed it half in and half out of the chest with the padlock.

Lastly, she secured the door with a great crossbeam fastened in the jambs, so that the witches could not enter.

Having done these things she waited.

Not long were the witches in coming back, and they raged and called for vengeance. "Open! Open!" they screamed. "Open, feet-water!"

"I cannot," said the feet-water. "I am scattered on the ground and my path is down to the Lough."

"Open, open, wood and trees and beam!" they cried to the door.

"I cannot," said the door. "For the beam is fixed in the jambs and I have no power to move."

"Open, open, cake that we have made and mingled with blood!" they cried again.

"I cannot," said the cake. "For I am broken and bruised, and my blood is on the lips of the sleeping children."
The witches rushed through the air with great cries, and fled back to Slievenamon, uttering strange curses on the Spirit of the Well, who had wished their ruin. But the woman and the house were left in peace, and a mantle dropped by one of the witches in her flight was kept hung up by the mistress in memory of that night. And this mantle was kept by the same family from generation to generation for five hundred years after.

5.

THE BIRTH OF OISÍN

ONE DAY as Finn, his companions and dogs were returning from the chase to their *Dún* on the Hill of Allen, a beautiful fawn started up on their path. The chase swept after her, she taking the way which led to their home. Soon, all the pursuers were left far behind save only Finn himself and his two hounds, Bran and Sceolaun. Now these hounds were of strange breed, for Tyren, sister to Murna, the mother of Finn, had been changed into a hound by the enchantment of a woman of the Faery Folk, who loved Tyrin's husband Ullan. The two hounds of Finn were the children of Tyren, born to her in that shape. Of all hounds in Ireland they were the best, and Finn loved them much, so that it was said he wept but twice in his life, and once was for the death of Bran.

At last, as the chase went on down a valley side, Finn saw the fawn stop and lie down, while the two hounds began to play round her and to lick her face and limbs. So he gave commandment that none should hurt her, and she followed them to the *Dún* of Allen, playing with the hounds as she went.

The same night Finn awoke and saw standing by his bed the fairest woman his eyes had ever beheld.

"I am Saba, oh Finn," she said, "and I was the fawn you chased today. Because I would not give my love to the Druid of the Faery Folk, who is named the Dark, he put that shape upon me by his sorceries, and I have borne it these three years. But a slave of his, pitying me, once revealed to me that if I could win to thy great *Dún* of Allen, oh Finn, I should be safe from all enchantments and my natural shape would come to me again. But I feared to be torn to pieces by thy dogs, or wounded by thy hunters, till at last I let myself be overtaken by thee alone and by Bran and Sceolaun, who have the nature of man and would do me no hurt."

"Have no fear, maiden," said Finn, "we the Fianna, are free and our guest-friends are free. There is none who shall put compulsion on you here."

So Saba dwelt with Finn and he made her his wife. So deep was his love for her that neither the battle nor the chase had any delight for him, and for months he never left her side. She also loved him as deeply, and their joy in each other was like that of the Immortals in the Land of Youth.

But at last word came to Finn that the warships of the Northmen were in the bay of Dublin, and he summoned his heroes to the fight.

"For," said he to Saba, "the men of Erin give us tribute and hospitality to defend them from the foreigner, and it were shame to take it from them and not to give that to which we, on our side, are pledged." And he called to mind that great saying of Goll mac Morna when they were once sore bested by a mighty host. "A man," said Goll, "lives after his life but not after his honor."

Seven days was Finn absent, and he drove the Northmen from the shores of Erin. But on the eighth day he returned, and when he entered his *Dún* he saw trouble in the eyes of his men and of their fair womenfolk, and Saba was not on the rampart expecting his return. So he bade them tell him what had chanced, and they said:

"Wilst thou, our father and lord, wert afar off smiting

the foreigner, and Saba looking ever down the pass for thy return, we saw one day as it were the likeness of thee approaching, and Bran and Sceolaun at thy heels. And we seemed also to hear the notes of the Fian hunting call blown on the wind. Then Saba hastened to the great gate, and we could not stay her, so eager was she to rush to the phantom. But when she came near, she halted and gave a loud and bitter cry, and the shape of thee smote her with a hazel wand, and lo, there was no woman there anymore, but a deer. Then those hounds chased it, and ever as it strove to reach again the gate of the *Dún* they turned it back. We all now seized what arms we could and ran out to drive away the enchanter, but when we reached the place there was nothing to be seen, only still we heard the rushing of flying feet and the baying of dogs, and one thought it came from here, and another from there, till at last the uproar died away and all was still. What we could do, oh Finn, we did. Saba is gone."

Finn then struck his hand on his breast but spoke no word, and he went to his own chamber. No man saw him for the rest of that day, nor for the day after. Then he came forth, and ordered the matters of the Fianna as of old, but for seven years thereafter he went searching for Saba through every remote glen and dark forest and cavern of Ireland, and he would take no hounds with him save Bran and Sceolaun. But at last he renounced all hope of finding her again, and went hunting as of old. One day as he was following the chase on Ben Gulban in Sligo, he heard the musical bay of the dogs change of a sudden to a fierce growling and yelping as though they were in combat with some beast, and running hastily up he and his men beheld, under a great tree, a naked boy with long hair, and around him the hounds struggling to seize him, but Bran and Sceolaun fighting with them and keeping them off. And the lad was tall and shapely, and as the heroes gathered round he gazed undauntedly on them, never heeding the rout of dogs at his feet. The Fians beat off the dogs and brought the lad home with them, and Finn was very silent and continually searched the lad's countenance with his eyes. In time, the use of speech came to him, and the story that he told was this:

He had known no father, and no mother save a gentle hind with whom he lived in a most green and pleasant valley shut in on every side by towering cliffs that could not be scaled, or by deep chasms in the earth. In the summer he lived on fruits and such-like, and in the winter, store of provisions was laid for him in a cave. And there came to them sometimes a tall dark-visaged man, who spoke to his mother, now tenderly, and now in loud menace, but she always shrunk away in fear, and the man departed in anger. At last there came a day when the Dark Man spoke very long with his mother in all tones of entreaty and of tenderness and of rage, but she would still keep aloof and give no sign save of fear and abhorrence. Then at length the Dark Man drew near and smote her with a hazel wand; and with that he turned and went his way, but she, this time, followed him, still looking back at her son and piteously complaining. And he, when he strove to follow, found himself unable to move a limb; and crying out with rage and desolation he fell to the earth and his senses left him. When he came to himself he was on the mountain side, on Ben Gulban, where he remained some days, searching for that green and hidden valley, which he never found again. And after a while the dogs found him; but of the hind his mother and of the Dark Druid, there is no man knows the end.

Finn called his name Oisín, and he became a warrior of fame, but far more famous for the songs and tales that he made; so that of all things to this day that are told of the Fianna of Erin, men are wont to say, "So sang the bard, Oisín, son of Finn."

6.

THE THIRTEENTH SON OF
THE KING OF ERIN

THERE WAS a king in Erin long ago who had thirteen sons, and as they grew up he taught them good learning and every exercise and art befitting their rank.

One day the king went hunting, and saw a swan swimming in a lake with thirteen little ones. She kept driving away the thirteenth and would not let it come near the others.

The king wondered greatly at this, and when he came home he summoned his Sean dall Glic, an old blind sage. "I saw a great wonder today while out hunting: a swan with thirteen cygnets. She drove away the thirteenth continually, and kept the twelve with her. Tell me the cause and reason of this. Why should a mother hate her thirteenth little one, and guard the other twelve?"

"I will tell you," said the old blind sage. "All creatures on earth, whether beast or human, which have thirteen young, should put the thirteenth away. They should let it wander for itself through the world and find its fate, so that the will of Heaven may work upon it, and not come down on the others. Now you have thirteen sons, and you must give the thirteenth to the *Diachbha*."

"Then that is the meaning of the swan on the lake; I must give up my thirteenth son to the *Diachbha?*"

"It is. You must give up one of your thirteen sons."

"But how can I give one of them away when I am so fond of all... and which one shall it be?"

"I'll tell you what to do. When the thirteen come home tonight, shut the door against the last that comes."

Now one of the sons was slow, not so keen nor so sharp as another. The eldest, who was called Sean Ruadh, was the best, the hero of them all. And it happened that night that he came home last, and when he came his father shut the door against him. The boy raised his hands and asked, "Father, what are you going to do with me; what do you wish?"

"It is my duty," said his father, "to give one of my sons to the *Diachbha*. As you are the thirteenth, you must go."

"Well, give me my outfit for the road."

The outfit was brought. Sean Ruadh put it on, and then the father gave him a black-haired steed that could overtake the wind before him, and outstrip the wind behind. Sean Ruadh mounted the steed and hurried away. He went on each day without rest, and slept in the woods at night.

One morning he put on some old clothes that he had in a pack on the saddle, and leaving his horse in the woods, went aside to an opening. He was not long there when a king rode up and stopped before him.

"Who are you, and where are you going?" asked the king.

"Oh!" exclaimed Sean Ruadh. "I am astray. I do not know where to go, nor what I am to do."

"If that is how you are, I'll tell you what to do. Come with me."

"Why should I go with you?"

"Well, I have a great many cows, and I have no one to

go with them, no one to mind them. I am also in great trouble. My daughter will die a terrible death very soon."

"How will she die?" asked Sean Ruadh.

"There is an *urfeist*, a great serpent of the sea, a monster which must get a king's daughter to devour every seven years. Once in seven years this thing comes up out of the sea for its meat. The turn has now come to my daughter, and we don't know what day will the *urfeist* appear. The whole castle and all of us are in mourning for my wretched child."

"Perhaps someone will come to save her."

"Alas, there is a whole army of kings' sons who have come, and they all promise to save her. But I'm in dread none of them will face the *urfeist*."

Sean Ruadh agreed with the king to serve for seven years, and went home with him. Next morning Sean Ruadh drove out the king's cows to pasture.

Now there were three giants not far from the king's place. They lived in three castles in sight of each other, and every night each of these giants shouted just before going to bed. So loud was the shout that each let out of himself that the people heard it in all the country around.

Sean Ruadh drove the cattle up to one of the giant's land, pushed down the wall, and let them in. The grass was very high; three times better than any on the king's pastures.

As Sean Ruadh sat watching the cattle, a giant came running towards him and called out, "I don't know whether to put a pinch of you in my nose, or a bite of you in my mouth!"

"Bad luck to me," said Sean Ruadh, "if I came here but to take the life out of you!"

"How would you like to fight; on the gray stones, or with sharp swords?" asked the giant.

"I'll fight you on the gray stones, where your great legs will be going down, and mine standing high."

They faced one another then, and began to fight. At the first encounter Sean Ruadh put the giant down to his knees among the hard gray stones. At the second he put him to his waist, and at the third to his shoulders.

"Come, take me out of this!" cried the giant, "and I'll give you my castle and all I've got. I'll give you my sword of light that never fails to kill at a blow. I'll give you my black horse that can overtake the wind before, and outstrip the wind behind. These are all up there in my castle."

Sean Ruadh killed the giant and went up to the castle, where the housekeeper said to him, "Oh! It is you that are welcome. You have killed the dirty giant that was here. Come with me now till I show you all the riches and treasures." She opened the door of the giant's storeroom. "All these are yours. Here are the keys of the castle."

"Keep them till I come again, and wake me in the evening," said Sean Ruadh, lying down on the giant's bed.

He slept till evening; then the housekeeper roused him, and he drove the king's cattle home. The cows never gave so much milk as that night. They gave as much as in a whole week before.

Sean Ruadh met the king, and asked, "What news from your daughter?"

"The great serpent did not come today," replied the king. "But he may come tomorrow."

"Well, tomorrow he may not come till another day," said Sean Ruadh.

Now the king knew nothing of the strength of Sean Ruadh, who was bare-footed, ragged, and shabby.

The second morning Sean Ruadh put the king's cows in the second giant's land. Out came the second giant with the same questions and threats as the first, and Sean Ruadh spoke as on the day before.

They fell to fighting, and when the giant was to his

shoulders in the hard gray rocks, he said, "I'll give you my sword of light and my brown-haired horse if you'll spare my life."

"Where is your sword of light?" asked Sean Ruadh.

"It is hung tip over my bed."

Sean Ruadh ran to the giant's castle and took the sword, which screamed out when he seized it. He held it fast, hurried back to the giant, and asked, "How shall I try the edge of this sword?"

"Against a stick," was the reply.

"I see no stick better than your own head," said Sean Ruadh. With that he swept the head off the giant, went back to the castle and hung up the sword.

"Blessing to you," said the housekeeper. "You have killed the giant! Come now, and I'll show you his riches and treasures, which are yours forever."

Sean Ruadh found more treasure in this castle than in the first one. When he had seen all, he gave the keys to the housekeeper till he should need them. He slept as on the day before, and then drove the cows home in the evening.

The king said, "I have the luck since you came to me. My cows give three times as much milk today as they did yesterday."

"Well," said Sean Ruadh, "have you any account of the *urfeist?*"

"He didn't come today," replied the king. "But he may come tomorrow."

Sean Ruadh went out with the king's cows on the third day. He drove them to the third giant's land, who came out and fought a more desperate battle than either of the other two. But Sean Ruadh pushed him down among the gray rocks to his shoulders and killed him.

At the castle of the third giant he was received with gladness by the housekeeper. She showed him the treasures and gave him the keys, but he left the keys with her till he should need them. That evening the king's cows had more milk than ever before.

On the fourth day Sean Ruadh went out with the cows, but stopped at the first giant's castle. The housekeeper at his command brought out the dress of the giant, which was all black. He put on the giant's apparel, black as night, and girded on his sword of light. Then he mounted the black-haired steed, which overtook the wind before, and outstripped the wind behind, and rushing on between earth and sky, he never stopped till he came to the beach. There he saw hundreds upon hundreds of kings' sons, and champions, who were anxious to save the king's daughter, but were so frightened at the terrible *urfeist* that they would not go near her.

When he had seen the princess and the trembling champions, Sean Ruadh turned his black steed to the castle. Presently the king saw, riding between earth and sky, a splendid stranger, who stopped before him.

"What is it that I see on the shore?" asked the stranger. "Is it a fair, or some great meeting?"

"Haven't you heard?" asked the king. "A monster is coming to destroy my daughter today."

"No, I haven't heard anything," answered the stranger, who turned away and disappeared.

Soon, the black horseman was before the princess, who sat alone on a rock near the sea. As she looked at the stranger, she thought he was the finest man on earth, and her heart was cheered.

"Have you no one to save you?" he asked.

"No one."

"Will you let me lay my head on your lap till the *urfeist* comes? Then rouse me."

He put his head on her lap and fell asleep. While he slept,

the princess took three hairs from his head and hid them in her bosom. As soon as she had hidden the hairs, she saw the *urfeist* coming on the sea, great as an island, and throwing up water to the sky as he moved. She roused the stranger, who sprang up to defend her.

The *urfeist* came upon shore, and was advancing on the princess with mouth open and wide as a bridge, when the stranger stood before him and said, "This woman is mine; not yours!"

Then drawing his sword of light, he swept off the monster's head with a blow. But the head rushed back to its place, and grew on again. In a twinkle the *urfeist* turned and went back to the sea.

As he went, he said, "I'll be here again tomorrow, and swallow the whole world before me as I come."

"Well," answered the stranger, "maybe another will come to meet you."

Sean Ruadh mounted his black steed, and was gone before the princess could stop him. Sad was her heart when she saw him rush off between the earth and sky more swiftly than any wind. He went to the first giant's castle and put away his horse, clothes, and sword. Then he slept on the giant's bed till evening, when the housekeeper woke him, and he drove home the cows.

Meeting the king, he asked, "Well, how has your daughter fared today?"

"Oh! The *urfeist* came out of the sea to carry her away, but a wonderful black champion came riding between earth and sky and saved her."

"Who was he?"

"There is many a man who says he did it. But my daughter isn't saved yet, for the *urfeist* said he'd come tomorrow."

"Never fear; perhaps another champion will come

tomorrow."

Next morning Sean Ruadh drove the king's cows to the land of the second giant, where he left them feeding, and then went to the castle, where the housekeeper met him.

"You are welcome," she said. "I'm here before you, and all is well."

"Let the brown horse be brought. Let the giant's apparel and sword be ready for me," ordered Sean Ruadh.

The apparel was brought, the beautiful blue dress of the second giant, and his sword of light. Sean Ruadh put on the apparel and took the sword. He mounted the brown steed, and sped away between earth and air three times more swiftly than the day before.

He rode first to the seashore, saw the king's daughter sitting on the rock alone, and the princes and champions far away, trembling in dread of the *urfeist*. Then he rode to the king, enquired about the crowd on the seashore, and received the same answer as before.

"But is there no man to save her?" asked Sean Ruadh.

"There are men enough," answered the king, "who promise to save her, and say they are brave. But there is no man of them who will stand to his word and face the *urfeist* when he rises from the sea."

Sean Ruadh was away before the king knew it, and rode to the princess in his suit of blue, bearing his sword of light. "Is there no one to save you?" asked he.

"No one."

"Let me lay my head on your lap, and when the *urfeist* comes, rouse me."

He put his head on her lap, and while he slept she took out the three hairs, compared them with his hair, and said to herself, "You are the man who was here yesterday."

When the *urfeist* appeared, coming over the sea, the princess roused the stranger, who sprang up and hurried to the beach.

The monster, moving at a greater speed, and raising more water than on the day before, came with open mouth to land. Again Sean Ruadh stood in his way, and with one blow of the giant's sword made two halves of the *urfeist*. But the two halves rushed together, and were one as before.

Then the *urfeist* turned to the sea again, and said as he went, "All the champions on earth won't save her from me tomorrow!"

Sean Ruadh sprang to his steed and back to the castle. He went, leaving the princess in despair at his going. She tore her hair and wept for the loss of the blue champion, the one man who had dared to save her.

Sean Ruadh put on his old clothes, and drove home the cows as usual.

The king said, "A strange champion, all dressed in blue, saved my daughter today. But she is grieving her life away because he is gone."

"Well, that is a small matter, since her life is safe," said Sean Ruadh.

There was a feast for the whole world that night at the king's castle, and gladness was on every face that the king's daughter was safe again.

Next day Sean Ruadh drove the cows to the third giant's pasture, went to the castle, told the housekeeper to bring the giant's sword and apparel, and have the red steed led to the door. The third giant's dress had as many colors as there are in the sky, and his boots were of blue glass. Sean Ruadh, dressed and mounted on his red steed, was the most beautiful man in the world.

When ready to start, the housekeeper said, "The beast will be so enraged this time that no arms can stop him. He will rise from the sea with three great swords coming out of his mouth, and he could cut to pieces and swallow the whole world if it stood before him in battle. There is only one way to conquer the *urfeist,* and I will show it to you. Take this brown apple, put it in your bosom, and when he comes rushing from the sea with open mouth, do you throw the apple down his throat. The great *urfeist* will melt away and die on the strand."

Sean Ruadh went on the red steed between earth and sky, with thrice the speed of the day before. He saw the maiden sitting on the rock alone, and the trembling kings' sons in the distance watching to know what would happen. He saw the king hoping for someone to save his daughter. He went to the princess, and put his head on her lap. When he had fallen asleep, she took the three hairs from her bosom, and looking at them, said, "You are the man who saved me yesterday."

The urfeist was not long in coming. The princess roused Sean Ruadh, who sprang to his feet and went to the sea. The urfeist came up enormous, terrible to look at, with a mouth big enough to swallow the world, and three sharp swords coming out of it. When he saw Sean Ruadh, he sprang at him with a roar. Sean Ruadh threw the apple into his mouth, and the beast fell helpless on the strand, flattened out and melted away to a dirty jelly on the shore.

Then Sean Ruadh went to the princess. "That urfeist will never trouble man or woman again."

The princess ran and tried to cling to him, but he was on the red steed, rushing away between earth and sky before she could stop him. She held, however, so firmly to one of the blue glass boots that Sean Ruadh had to leave it in her hands.

When he drove home the cows that night, the king came out, and Sean Ruadh asked, "What news from the urfeist?"

"Oh," said the king, "I've had the luck since you came to me. A champion wearing all the colors of the sky, and riding a red steed between earth and air, destroyed the urfeist today. My daughter is safe forever. But she is ready to kill herself because she hasn't the man that saved her."

That night there was a feast in the king's castle such as no one had ever seen before. The halls were filled with princes and champions, and each one said, "I am the man that saved the princess!"

The king sent for the old blind sage, and asked what should he do to find the man who saved his daughter.

The old blind sage said, "Send out word to all the world that the man whose foot the blue glass boot will fit is the champion who killed the *urfeist*, and you'll give him your daughter in marriage."

The king sent out word to the world to come to try on the boot. It was too large for some, too small for others. When all had failed, the old sage said, "All have tried the boot but the cowherd."

"He is always out with the cows; what use in his trying," said the king.

"No matter," answered the old blind sage. "Let twenty men go and bring him down."

The king sent up twenty men, who found the cowherd sleeping in the shadow of a stone wall. They began to make a hay rope to bind him, but he woke up and had twenty ropes ready before they had one. Then he jumped at them, tied the twenty in a bundle, and fastened the bundle to the wall.

They waited and waited at the castle for the twenty men and the cowherd, till at last the king sent twenty men more, with swords, to know what was the delay.

When they came, this twenty began to make a hay rope to tie the cowherd. But he had twenty ropes made before their one, and no matter how they fought, the cowherd tied the twenty in a bundle, and the bundle to the other twenty men.

When neither party came back, the old blind sage said to

the king, "Go up now, and throw yourself down before the cowherd, for he has tied the forty men in two bundles, and the bundles to each other."

The king went and threw himself down before the cowherd, who raised him up and asked, "What is this for?"

"Come down now and try on the glass boot," said the king.

"How can I go, when I have work to do here?"

"Never mind; you'll come back soon enough to do the work."

The cowherd untied the forty men and went down with the king. When he stood in front of the castle, he saw the princess sitting in her upper chamber, and the glass boot on the windowsill before her.

That moment the boot sprang from the window through the air to him, and went on his foot of itself. The princess was downstairs in a twinkle, and in the arms of Sean Ruadh.

He saw the whole place was crowded with kings' sons and champions, who claimed that they had saved the princess. "What are these men here for?" he asked.

"They have been trying to put on the boot," replied the king.

With that Sean Ruadh drew his sword of light, swept the heads off every man of them, and threw heads and bodies on the dirt-heap behind the castle.

Then the king sent ships with messengers to all the kings and queens of the world. To the kings of Spain, France, Greece, and Lochlin, and to Diarmuid, son of the monarch of light. To come to the wedding of his daughter and Sean Ruadh.

After the wedding, Sean Ruadh went with his wife to live in the kingdom of the giants, and left his father-in-law on his own land.

7.

THE COMING OF FINN

AND NOW we tell how Finn came to the captaincy of the Fianna of Erin. At this time Ireland was ruled by one of the mightiest of her native kings, Conn, son of Felimy, who was surnamed Conn of the Hundred Battles. And Conn sat in his great banqueting hall at Tara, while the yearly Assembly of the lords and princes of the Gael went forward. During this it was the inviolable law that no quarrel should be raised and no weapon drawn, so that every man who had a right to come to that Assembly might come there and sit next his deadliest foe in peace.

Below him sat at meat the provincial kings and the chiefs of clans, and the High King's officers and fighting men of the Fianna, with Goll and the sons of Morna at their head. And there, too, sat modestly a strange youth, tall and fair, whom no one had seen in that place before. Conn marked him with the eye of a king that is accustomed to mark men, and by and by he sent him a horn full of wine from his own table and bade the youth declare his name and lineage.

"I am Finn, son of Cuilll," said the youth, standing among them, tall as a warriors spear.

A start and a low murmur ran through the Assembly while the captains of the Fianna stared upon him, like men who see a vision of the dead.

"What seek you here?" asked Conn.

Finn replied, "To be your man, O King, and to do you service in war as my father did."

"It is well," said the King. "Thou art a friend's son and the son of man of trust."

So Finn put his hand in the Kind's and swore fealty and service to him, and Conn set him beside his own son Art, and all fell to talking again and wondering what new things that day would bring forth, and the feasting went merrily forward.

Now, at this time the people of the royal burg of Tara were sorely afflicted by a goblin of the Faery Folk, who was wont to approach the place at nightfall, there to work what harm to man, or beast, or dwelling that he found in his evil mind to do. And he could not be resisted, for as he came he played on a magic harp a strain so keen and sweet, that each man who heard it must needs stand entranced and motionless until the faery music had passed away.

The King proclaimed a mighty reward to any man who would save Tara from the goblin, and Finn thought in his heart, "I am the man to do that." So he said to the King, "Shall I have my rightful heritage as captain of the Fianna of Erin if I slay the goblin?"

Conn said, "I promise thee that," and he bound himself by the sureties of all the provincial Kings of Ireland and of the Druid Kithro and his magicians.

Now, there was among the following of Conn a man named Fiacha, who had been as a youth a trusty friend and follower of Cuilll. He came to Finn and brought with him a spear having a head of dark bronze with glittering edges. It was fastened with thirty rivets of Arabian gold, and the spearhead was laced up within a leathern case.

"By this weapon of enchantment," said Fiacha, "you shall overcome the enchanter." He taught Finn what to do with it when the hour of need should come.

So Finn took the spear, and left the strings of the case loose, and he paced with it towards nightfall around the ramparts of royal Tara. When he had once made the circuit of the rampart and the light had now almost quite faded from the summer sky, and the wide low plains around the Hill of Tara were a sea of white mist, he heard far off in the deepening gloom the first notes of the faery harp. Never such music was made by mortal hand, for it had in it sorrows that man has never felt, and joys for which man has no name. It seemed as if a man listening to that music might burst from time into eternity and be as one of the Immortals for evermore. And Finn listened, amazed and rapt, till at last as the triumphant melody grew nearer and louder he saw dimly a Shadow Shape playing as it were on a harp, and coming swiftly towards him.

With a mighty effort he roused himself from dreams, and tore the cover from the spearhead and laid the metal to his brow. The demoniac energy that had been beaten into the blade by the hammers of unearthly craftsmen in ancient days thrilled through him and made him fighting-mad. He rushed forward, shouting his battle cry, and swinging the spear aloft. But the Shadow turned and fled before him, and Finn chased it northward to the Faery Mound of Slieve Fuad, and there he drove the spear through its back.

And what it was that fell there in the night, and what it was that passed like the shadow of a shadow into the Faery Mound, none can tell. But Finn bore back with him next day a pale, sorrowful head on the point of Fiacha's spear, and the goblin troubled the folk of royal Tara no more.

But Conn of the Hundred Battles called the Fianna

together, and he set Finn at his right hand. "Here is your Captain by birthright and by sword-right," he proclaimed. "Let who will now obey him henceforward, and who will not, let him go in peace and serve Arthur of Britain or Arist of Alba, or whatsoever King he will."

Goll, son of Morna, said, "For my part I will be Finn's man under thee, O King," and he swore obedience and loyalty to Finn before them all.

Nor was it hard for any man to step where Goll had gone before. They all took their oaths of Fian service to Finn mac Cuill. And thus it was that Finn came to the captaincy of the Fianna of Erin, and he ruled the Fianna many a year till he died in battle with the Clan Urgrenn at Brea upon the Boyne.

8.

FINN MAC CUILL AND THE FENIANS OF ERIN IN THE CASTLE OF FEAR DUBH

IT WAS the custom with Finn mac Cuill and the Fenians of Erin, when a stranger from any part of the world came to their castle, not to ask him a question for a year and a day.

On a time, a champion came to Finn and his men, and remained with them. He was not at all pleasant or agreeable. At last Finn and his men took counsel together. They were much annoyed because their guest was so dull and morose, never saying a word, always silent.

While discussing what kind of man he was, Diarmuid Duivne offered to try him, so one evening when they were eating together, Diarmuid came and snatched from his mouth the hind-quarter of a bullock, at which he was picking.

Diarmuid pulled at one part of the quarter with all his strength, but only took the part that he seized, while the other kept the part he held. All laughed; the stranger laughed too, as heartily as any. It was the first laugh they had heard from him.

The strange champion saw all their feats of arms and

practiced with them, till the year and a day were over. Then he said to Finn and his men, "I have spent a pleasant year in your company. You gave me good treatment, and the least I can do now is to give you a feast at my own castle."

No one had asked what his name was up to that time. Finn now asked his name. He answered, "My name is Fear Dubh, of Alba."

Finn accepted the invitation. They appointed the day for the feast, which was to be in Erin, since Fear Dubh did not wish to trouble them to go to Alban. He took leave of his host and started for home.

When the day for the feast came, Finn and the chief men of the Fenians of Erin set out for the castle of Fear Dubh.

They went, a glen at a step, a hill at a leap, and thirty-two miles at a running leap, till they came to the grand castle where the feast was to be given.

Everything was ready. Seats at the table, and every man's name at his seat in the same order as at Finn's castle. Diarmuid, who was always very sportive, fond of hunting, and paying court to women, was not with them. He had gone to the mountains with his dogs.

All sat down, except Conan Maol mac Morna, who never a man spoke well of. No seat was ready for him, for he used to lie on the flat of his back on the floor at Finn's castle.

When all were seated the door of the castle closed of itself. Finn asked the man nearest the door to rise and open it. The man tried to rise. He pulled this way and that, over and hither, but he couldn't get up. Then the next man tried, and the next, and so on, till the turn came to Finn himself, who tried in vain.

Now, whenever Finn and his men were in trouble and great danger it was their custom to raise a cry of distress, heard all over Erin. Then all men knew that they were in peril of death. They never raised this cry except in the last extremity.

Finn's son, Fialan, who was three years old and in the cradle, heard the cry, was roused, and jumped up. "Get me a sword!" said he to the nurse. "My father and his men are in distress; I must go to aid them."

"What could you do, poor little child?"

Fialan looked around and saw an old rusty sword blade laid aside for ages. He took it down and gave it a snap. It sprang up so as to hit his arm, and all the rust dropped off. The blade was pure as shining silver.

"This will do," said he, and then set out towards the place where he heard the cry. He went a glen at a step, a hill at a leap, and thirty-two miles at a running leap, till he came to the door of the castle, and cried out.

Finn answered from inside. "Is that you, my child?"

"It is," said Fialan.

"Why did you come?"

"I heard your cry, and how could I stay at home, hearing the cry of my father and the Fenians of Erin!"

"Oh, my child, you cannot help us much."

Fialan struck the door powerfully with his sword, but no use. One of the men inside asked Finn to chew his thumb, to know what was keeping them in, and why they were bound. Finn chewed his thumb, from skin to blood, from blood to bone, from bone to marrow, and discovered that Fear Dubh had built the castle by magic. He was coming himself with a great force to cut the head off each one of them. The men of Alba had always a grudge against the champions of Erin.

Said Finn to Fialan, "Do you go now, and stand at the ford near the castle, and meet Fear Dubh."

Fialan went and stood in the middle of the ford. He wasn't long there when he saw Fear Dubh coming with a great army.

"Leave the ford, my child," said Fear Dubh, who knew him at once. "I have not come to harm your father. I spent a pleasant year at his castle. I've only come to show him honor."

"I know why you have come," answered Fialan. "You've come to destroy my father and all his men, and I'll not leave this ford while I can hold it."

"Leave the ford. I don't want to harm your father; I want to do him honor. If you don't let us pass my men will kill you."

"I will not let you pass so long as I'm alive before you," said Fialan.

The men faced him and a battle commenced, the like of which was never seen before that day. Fialan went through the army as a hawk through a flock of sparrows on a March morning, till he killed every man except Fear Dubh. Fear Dubh told him again to leave the ford; he didn't want to harm his father.

"Oh!" said Fialan, "I know well what you want."

"If you don't leave this place I'll make you leave it," said Fear Dubh.

Then they closed in combat, and such a combat was never seen before between any two warriors. They made springs to rise through the center of hard gray rocks, cows to cast their calves whether they had them or not. All the horses of the country were racing about and neighing in dread and fear, and all created things were terrified at the sound and clamor of the fight. At last the weapons of Fear Dubh went to pieces in the struggle, and Fialan made two halves of his own sword.

Now they closed in, wrestling. In the first round Fialan put Fear Dubh to his knees in the hard bottom of the river. The second round he put him to his hips, and the third, to his shoulders.

"Now," said he, "I have you." He gave him a stroke of the half of his sword, which cut the head off him. Then Fialan went to the door of the castle and told his father what he had done.

Finn chewed his thumb again, and knew what other danger was coming. "My son," said he to Fialan. "Fear Dubh has a younger brother more powerful than he was. That brother is coming against us now with greater forces than those which you have destroyed."

As soon as Fialan heard these words he hurried to the ford, and waited till the second army came up. He destroyed this army as he had the other, and closed with the second brother in a fight fiercer and more terrible than the first. At last he thrust him to his armpits in the hard bottom of the river and cut off his head. Then he went to the castle and told his father what he had done.

A third time Finn chewed his thumb. "My son, a third army more to be dreaded than the other two is coming now to destroy us. At the head of it is the youngest brother of Fear Dubh, the most desperate and powerful of the three."

Again Fialan rushed off to the ford, and though the work was greater than before, he left not a man of the army alive. Then he closed with the youngest brother of Fear Dubh, and if the first and second battles were terrible this was more terrible by far. But at last he planted the youngest brother up to his armpits in the hard bottom of the river, and swept the head off him.

Now, after the heat and struggle of combat, Fialan was in such a rage that he lost his mind from fury, not having any one to fight against. If the whole world had been there before him he would have gone through it and conquered it all. But having no one to face him he rushed along the river bank, tearing the flesh from his own body. Never had such madness been seen in any created being before that day.

Diarmuid came now and knocked at the door of the castle, having the dog Bran with him, and asked Finn what had caused him to raise the cry of distress.

"Oh, Diarmuid," said Finn. "We are all fastened in here to be killed. Fialan has destroyed three armies, and Fear Dubh with his two brothers. He is raging now along the bank of the river. You must not go near him, for he would tear you limb from limb. At this moment he wouldn't spare me, his own father. But after a while he will cease from raging and die down; then you can go. The mother of Fear Dubh is coming, and will soon be at the ford. She is more violent, more venomous, more to be dreaded, a greater warrior than her sons. The chief weapon she has are the nails on her fingers. Each nail is seven perches long, of the hardest steel on earth. She is coming in the air at this moment with the speed of a hawk, and she has a *kŭŕan* containing liquor inside, which has such power that if she puts three drops of it on the mouths of her sons they will rise up as well as ever. If she brings them to life there is nothing to save us.

"Go to the ford; she will be hovering over the corpses of the three armies to know can she find her sons, and as soon as she sees them she will dart down and give them the liquor. You must rise with a mighty bound upon her, dash the *kŭŕan* out of her hand and spill the liquor.

"If you can kill her, save her blood, for nothing in the world can free us from this place and open the door of the castle but the blood of the old hag. I'm in dread you'll not succeed, for she is far more terrible than all her sons together. Go now. Fialan is dying away, and the old woman is coming. Make no delay."

Diarmuid hurried to the ford, stood watching a while, then he saw high in the air something no larger than a hawk. As it came nearer and nearer he saw it was the old woman. She hovered high in the air over the ford. At last she saw her sons, and was swooping down when Diarmuid rose with a bound into the air and struck the vial a league out of her hand.

The old hag gave a shriek that was heard to the eastern world, and screamed, "Who has dared to interfere with me or my sons?"

"I," answered Diarmuid. "And you'll not go further till I do to you what has been done to your sons."

The fight began, and if there ever was a fight, before or since, it could not be more terrible than this one. But great as was the power of Diarmuid he never could have conquered but for Bran the dog.

The old woman with her nails stripped the skin and flesh from Diarmuid almost to the vitals. But Bran tore the skin and flesh off the old woman's back from her head to her heels. From the dint of blood-loss and fighting, Diarmuid was growing faint. Despair came on him, and he was on the point of giving way, when a little robin flew near to him, and sitting on a bush, spoke.

"Oh, Diarmuid, take strength. Rise and sweep the head off the old hag, or Finn and the Fenians of Erin are no more."

Diarmuid took courage. With his last strength he made one great effort, swept the head off the old hag and caught her blood in a vessel. He rubbed some on his own wounds. They were cured; then he cured Bran.

Straightway he took the blood to the castle, rubbed drops of it on the door, which opened, and he went in. All laughed with joy at the rescue. He freed Finn and his men by rubbing the blood on the chairs, but when he came as far as Conan Maol the blood gave out. All were going away.

"Why should you leave me here after you?" cried Conan Maol. "I would rather die at once than stay here for a lingering death. Why don't you, Oscar, and you, Gol mac

Morna, come and tear me out of this place. Anyhow you'll be able to drag the arms out of me and kill me at once. Better that than leave me to die alone."

Oscar and Gol took each a hand, braced their feet against his feet, put forth all their strength and brought him standing. But he left all the skin and much of the flesh from the back of his head to his heels on the floor behind him. He was covered with blood, and by all accounts was in a terrible condition, bleeding and wounded.

Now, there were sheep grazing near the castle. The Fenians ran out, killed and skinned the largest and best of the flock, and clapped the fresh skin on Conan's back. Such was the healing power in the sheep, and the wound very fresh, that Conan's back healed. He marched home with the rest of the men, and soon got well. And every year they sheared off his back wool enough to make a pair of stockings for each one of the Fenians of Erin, and for Finn himself.

And that was a great thing to do and useful, for wool was scarce in Erin in those days. Finn and his men lived pleasantly and joyously for some time. And if they didn't, may we.

9.

THE VENGEANCE
OF MESGEDRA

ATHARNA THE Bard, surnamed the Extortionate, was the chief poet and satirist of Ulster in the reign of Conor mac Nessa. Greed and arrogance were in his heart and poison on his tongue. The kings and lords of whom he asked rewards for his poems dared not refuse him aught, partly because of the poisonous satires and lampoons that he would otherwise make upon them for their avariciousness, and partly for in Ireland at that day it was deemed shameful to refuse to a bard whatsoever he might ask. Once it was said that he asked of a king named Eochy mac Luchta, who was famed for hospitality and generosity, the single thing that Eochy would have been grieved to give: namely his eye, and Eochy had but one eye. But the King plucked it out by the roots and gave it to him, and Atharna went away disappointed, for he had hoped that Eochy would ransom his eye at a great price.

Now, Conor mac Nessa, King of Ulster, and all the Ulster lords, having grown very powerful and haughty, became ill neighbors to all the other kingdoms in Ireland. On fertile Leinster above all they fixed their eyes, and sought for an opportunity to attack and plunder the province. Conor resolved at last to move Atharna to go to the King of Leinster, in the hope that he himself might be rid of Atharna. The King of Leinster might kill him for his insolence and his exactions, and then Conor might avenge the death of his bard by the invasion of Leinster.

Atharna therefore set out for Leinster accompanied by his train of poets, harpers and gillies and arrived at the great *Dún* of Mesgedra the King, at Naas in Kildare. Here he dwelt for twelve months wasting the substance of the Leinstermen. In the end when he was minded to return to Ulster he went before the King Mesgedra and the lords of Leinster and demanded his poet's fee.

"What is thy demand, Atharna?" asked Mesgedra.

"So many cattle and so many sheep," answered Atharna. "And store of gold and raiment, and of the fairest dames and maidens of Leinster forty-five, to grind at my querns in *Dún* Atharna."

"It shall be granted thee," said the King.

Then Atharna feared some mischief, for the King and the nobles of Leinster had not seemed like men on whom shameful conditions are laid, nor had they offered to ransom their women. Atharna therefore judged that the Leinstermen might fall upon him to recover their booty when he was once beyond the border, for within their own borders they might not affront a guest. He sent, therefore, a swift messenger to Conor mac Nessa, bidding him come with a strong escort as quickly as he might, to meet Atharna's band on the marches of Leinster, and convey him safely home.

Atharna then departed from Naas with a great herd of sheep and cattle and other spoils, and with thrice fifteen of the noble women of Leinster. He went leisurely, meaning to strike the high road to Emania from Dublin. When he came thither the Liffey was swollen with rain, and the ford at Dublin might not be crossed. He caused, therefore, many great hurdles to be made, and these were set in the river. Over them a causeway of boughs was laid, so that his cattle and spoils came safely across. Hence is the town of that place called to this day in Gaelic the City of the Hurdle Ford.

On the next day Conor and the Ulstermen met him, but a great force of the men of Leinster was also marching from Naas to the border, to recover their womenfolk, even as Atharna had expected. The Leinstermen then broke the battle on the company from Ulster, and defeated them, driving them with the cows of Atharna on to the sea cape of Ben Edar, known today as Howth, but they recovered the women. On Ben Edar did King Conor with the remnant of his troop then fortify themselves, making a great push across the neck of land by which Ben Edar is joined to the mainland. Here they were besieged; with hard fighting by day and night, expecting that help should come to them from Ulster, whither they had sent messengers to tell of their distress.

Now, Conall of the Victories was left behind to rule in Emania when Conor set forth to Leinster. He now, on hearing how the King was beset, assembled a great host and marched down to Ben Edar. Here he attacked the host of Leinster, and a great battle was fought, many being slain on both sides. The King of Leinster, Mesgedra, lost his left hand in the fight. In the end the men of Leinster were routed, and fled, and Mesgedra drove in his chariot past the City of the Hurdle Ford and Naas to the fords of Liffey at Clane. Here there was a sacred oak tree where druid rites and worship were performed. That oak tree was sanctuary, so that within its shadow, guarded by mighty spells, no man might be slain by his enemy.

Now Conall Cearnach had followed hard on the track of Mesgedra. When he found him beneath the oak, he drove his chariot round and round the circuit of the sanctuary, bidding Mesgedra come forth and do battle with him, or be counted a dastard among the kings of Erin.

Mesgedra said, "Is it the fashion of the champions of Ulster to challenge one-armed men to battle?"

Conall let his charioteer bind one of his arms to his side, and again he taunted Mesgedra and bade him come forth.

Mesgedra then drew sword, and between him and Conall there was a fierce fight until the Liffey was reddened with their blood. At last, by a chance blow of the sword of Mesgedra, the bonds of Conall's left arm were severed.

"On thy head be it," said Conall, "if thou release me again."

Then he caused his arm to be bound up once more, and again they met, sword to sword, and again in the fury of the fight Mesgedra cut the thongs that bound Conall's arm.

"The gods themselves have doomed thee!" shouted Conall, and he rushed upon Mesgedra and in no long time he wounded him to death.

"Take my head," said Mesgedra then, "and add my glory to thy glory, but be well assured this wrong shall yet be avenged by me upon Ulster," and he died.

Then Conall cut off the head of Mesgedra and put it in his chariot. Taking the chariot of Mesgedra he fared northwards. Ere long he met a chariot and fifty women accompanying it. In it was Buan the Queen, wife of Mesgedra, returning from a visit to Meath.

"Who art thou, woman?" asked Conall.

"I am Buan, wife of Mesgedra the King."

"Thou art to come with me," ordered Conall.

"Who hath commanded this?" said Buan.

"Mesgedra the King."

"By what token dost thou lay these commands upon me?"

"Behold his chariot and his horses."

"He gives rich gifts to many a man," answered the Queen.

Then Conall showed her the head of her husband. "This is my token," said he.

"It is enough," said Buan. "But give me leave to bewail him ere I go into captivity." Then she rose up in her chariot and raised for Mesgedra a keen of sorrow so loud and piercing that her heart broke with it. She fell backwards on the road and died.

Conall Cearnach then buried her there, and laid the head of her husband by her side. The fair hazel tree that grew from her grave by the fords of Clane was called Coll Buana, or the Hazel Tree of Buan.

But ere Conall buried the head of Mesgedra he caused the brain to be taken out and mixed with lime to make a bullet for a sling. It was customary to do when a great warrior had been killed, and the brain-bullet thus made were accounted to be the deadliest of missiles.

So when Leinster had been harried and plundered and its king and queen thus slain, the Ulstermen drew northward again, and the brain-bullet was laid up in the *Dún* of King Conor at Emania.

Years afterwards it happened that the Wolf of Connacht, namely Ket, son of Maga, came disguised within the borders of Ulster in search of prey, and he entered the palace precincts of Conor in Emania. There he saw two jesters of the King, who had got the brain-bullet from the shelf where it lay, and were rolling it about the courtyard. Ket knew it for what it was, and put it out of sight of the jesters and took it away with him while they made search for it. Thenceforth Ket carried it ever about with him in his girdle, hoping that he might yet use it to destroy some great warrior among the Ulstermen.

One day thereafter Ket made a foray on the men of Ross, and carried away a spoil of cattle. The host of Ulster and King Conor with them overtook him as he went homeward.

The men of Connacht had also mustered to the help of Ket, and both sides made them ready for battle. Now a river, namely Brosna, ran between them. On a hill at one side of this were assembled a number of the noble women of Connacht, who desired greatly to look on the far-famed Ultonian warriors, and above all on Conor the King, whose presence was said to be royal and stately beyond any man that was then living in Erin. Among the bushes, close to the women, Ket hid himself, and lay still but watchful.

Now Conor, seeing none but womenfolk close to him at this point, and being willing to show them his splendor, drew near to the bank on his side of the stream. Then Ket leaped up, whirling his sling, and the bullet hummed across the river and smote King Conor on the temple. His men carried him off for dead, and the men of Connacht broke the battle on the Ultermen, slaying many, and driving the rest of them back to their own place. This battle was thenceforth called the Battle of the Ford of the Sling-cast, or Athnurchar, and so the place is called to this day.

When Conor was brought home to Emania, his chief physician, Fingen, found the bullet half buried in his temple. "If the bullet be taken out," said he, "he will die. If it remain he will live, but he will bear the blemish of it."

"Let him bear the blemish," said the Ulster lords. "That is a small matter compared with the death of Conor."

Then Fingen stitched the wound over with a thread of gold, for Conor had curling golden hair, and bade him keep himself from all violent movements and from all vehement passions, and not to ride on horseback, and he would do well.

After that Conor lived for seven years, and he went not to war during that time, and all cause of passion was kept far from him. Then one day at broad noon the sky darkened, and the gloom of night seemed to spread over the world. All the people feared, and looked for some calamity. Conor called to him his chief druid, namely Bacarach, and inquired of him as to the cause of the gloom.

The druid then went with Conor into a sacred grove of oaks and performed the rites of divination. In a trance he spoke to Conor, saying, "I see a hill near a great city, and three high crosses on it. To one of them is nailed the form of a young man who is like unto one of the Immortals. Round him stand soldiers with tall spears, and a great crowd waiting to see him die."

"Is he, then, a malefactor?"

"Nay," said the druid, "but holiness, innocence, and truth have come to earth in him. For this cause have the druids of his land doomed him to die, for his teaching was not as theirs. And the heavens are darkened for wrath and sorrow at the sight."

Then Conor leaped up in a fury, crying, "They shall not slay him, they shall not slay him! Would I were there with the host of Ulster, and thus would I scatter his foes." With that he snatched his sword and began striking at the trees that stood thickly about him in the druid grove. Then with the heat of his passion the sling-bullet burst from his head, and he fell to the ground and died.

Thus was fulfilled the vengeance of Mesgedra upon Conor mac Nessa, King of Ulster.

10.

THE DEATH SIGN

A WOMAN was out one day looking after her sheep in the valley.

Coming by a little stream she sat down to rest, when suddenly she seemed to hear the sound of low music.

Turning round, she beheld at some distance a crowd of people dancing and making merry. She grew afraid and turned her head away not to see them.

Then close by her stood a young man, pale and strange looking, and she beheld him with fear.

"Who are you?" she said at last. "Why do you stand beside me?"

"You ought to know me," he replied. "For I belong to this place. Make haste now and come away, or evil will befall you."

She stood up and was going away with him, when the crowd left off their dancing and ran towards them crying, "Come back! Come back! Come back!"

"Don't stop; don't listen," said the young man. "Follow me."

They both began to run, and ran on until they reached a hillock. "Now we are safe," said he. "They can't harm us here."

When they stopped he said to her again, "Look me in the face and say if you know me now?"

"No," she answered, "you are a stranger to me."

"Look again. Look me straight in the face and you will know me."

She looked, and knew instantly that he was a man who had been drowned the year before in the dark winter time, and the waves had never cast up his body on the shore.

She threw up her arms. "Have you news of my child? Have you seen her, my fair-haired girl that was stolen from me this day seven years? Will she come back to me never no more?"

"I have seen her," said the man, "but she will never come back, never more. For she has eaten of the faery food and must now stay with the spirits under the sea, for she belongs to them body and soul. But go home now, for it is late, and evil is near you. Perhaps you will meet her sooner than you think."

Then as the woman turned her face homeward, the man disappeared and she saw him no more.

When at last she reached the threshold of her house, a fear and trembling came on her. She called to her husband that someone stood in the doorway and she could not pass. And with that she fell down on the threshold on her face, but spake no word more. And when they lifted her up she was dead.

11.

THE SECRET OF LABRA

IN VERY ancient days there was a King in Ireland named Labra, who was called Labra the Sailor for a certain voyage that he made. Now, Labra was never seen save by one man, once a year, without a hood that covered his head and ears. But once a year it was his habit to let his hair be cropped, and the person to do this was chosen by lot, for the King was accustomed to put to death instantly the man who had cropped him.

And so it happened that on a certain year the lot fell on a young man who was the only son of a poor widow, who dwelt near by the palace of the King. When she heard that her son had been chosen she fell on her knees before the King and besought him, with tears, that her son, who was her only support and all she had in the world, might not suffer death as was customary.

The King was moved by her grief and her entreaties, and at last he consented that the young man should not be slain provided that he vowed to keep secret to the day of his death what he should see. The youth agreed to this and he vowed by the Sun and the Wind that he would never, so long as he lived, reveal to man what he should learn when he cropped the King's hair.

So he did what was appointed for him and went home.

But when he did so he had no peace, for the wonder of the secret that he had learned preyed upon his mind so that he could not rest for thinking of it. Longing to reveal it, at last he fell into a wasting sickness from it, and was near to die. Then there was brought to see him a wise druid, who was skilled in all maladies of the mind and body.

After he had talked with the youth he said to his mother, "Thy son is dying of the burden of a secret which he may not reveal to any man, but until he reveals it he will have no ease. Let him, therefore, walk along the highway till he comes to a place where four roads meet. Let him then turn to the right, and the first tree that he shall meet on the roadside let him tell the secret to it. So it may be he shall be relieved, and his vow will not be broken."

The mother told her son of the druid's advice, and next day he went upon his way till he came to four crossroads, and he took the road upon the right, and the first tree he found was a great willow-tree. So the young man laid his cheek against the bark, and he whispered the secret to the tree. As he turned back homeward he felt lightened of his burden, and he leaped and sang, and ere many days were past he was as well and light-hearted as ever he had been in his life.

Some while after that it happened that the King's harper, namely Craftiny, broke the straining-post of his harp and went out to seek for a piece of wood wherewith to mend it. And the first timber he found that would fit the purpose was the willow tree by the crossroads. He cut it down, therefore, and took as much as would give him a new straining-post, and bore it home with him and mended his harp with it.

That night he played after meat before the King and his lords as he was wont, but whatever he played and sang, the

folk that listened to him seemed to hear only one thing:

"Two horse's ears hath Labra the Sailor."

Then the King plucked off his hood, and after that he made no secret of his ears and none suffered on account of them thenceforward.

12.

THE KING OF ERIN'S SON
AND THE GIANT
OF LOCH LÉIN

ON A time there lived a king and a queen in Killarney in Erin, and they had an only son. They were very careful and fond of this son. Whatever he asked for was granted, and what he wanted he had.

When grown to be almost a young man the son went away one day to the hills to hunt. He could find no game, saw nothing all day. Towards evening he sat down on a hillside to rest, but soon stood up again and started to go home empty-handed. He heard a whistle behind him, and turning, saw a giant hurrying down the hill.

The giant came to him, took his hand, and said, "Can you play cards?"

"I can indeed," said the king's son.

"Well, if you can," said the giant, "we'll have a game here on this hillside."

So the two sat down, and the giant had out a pack of cards in a twinkling. "What shall we play for?" he asked.

"For two estates," answered the king's son.

They played. The young man won, and went home the better for two estates. He was very glad, and hurried to tell his father the luck he had.

Next day he went to the same place, and didn't wait long till the giant came again.

"Welcome, king's son," said the giant. "What shall we play for today?"

"I'll leave that to yourself," answered the young man.

"Well," said the giant. "I have five hundred bullocks with golden horns and silver hooves. I'll play them against as many cattle belonging to you."

"Agreed," said the king's son.

They played. The giant lost again. He had the cattle brought to the place, and the king's son went home with the five hundred bullocks. The king his father was outside watching, and was more delighted than the day before when he saw the drove of beautiful cattle with horns of gold and hooves of silver.

When the bullocks were driven in, the king sent for Sean dall Glic, the old blind sage, to know what he would say of the young man's luck.

"My advice," said the old blind sage, "is not to let your son go the way of the giant again. For if he plays with him a third time he'll rue it."

But nothing could keep the king's son from playing the third time. Away he went, in spite of every advice and warning, and sat on the same hillside. He waited long, but no one came. At last he rose to go home. That moment he heard a whistle behind him, and turning, saw the giant coming.

"Well, will you play with me today?" asked the giant.

"I would," said the king's son. "But I have nothing to bet."

"You have indeed."

"I have not."

"Haven't you your head?" asked the giant of Loch Léin, for it was he that was in it.

"I have," answered the king's son.

"So have I my head," said the giant. "We'll play for each other's heads."

This third time the giant won the game, and the king's son was to give himself up in a year and a day to the giant in his castle.

The young man went home sad and weary. The king and queen were outside watching, and when they saw him approaching, they knew great trouble was on him. When he came to where they were, he wouldn't speak, but went straight into the castle, and wouldn't eat or drink.

He was sad and lamenting for a good while, till at last he disappeared one day, the king and queen knew not whither. After that they didn't hear of him, didn't know was he dead or alive.

The young man after he left home walked along over the kingdom for a long time. One day he saw no house, big or little, till after dark. He came in front of a hill, and at the foot of the hill saw a small light. He went to the light, found a small house, and inside an old woman sitting at a warm fire. Every tooth in her head was as long as a staff.

She stood up when he entered, took him by the hand, and said, "You are welcome to my house, son of the king of Erin." Then she brought warm water, washed his feet and legs from the knees down, gave him supper, and put him to bed.

When he rose next morning he found breakfast ready before him. The old woman said, "You were with me last night; you'll be with my sister tonight. What she tells you to do or your head'll be in danger. Now, take the gift I give you. Here is a ball of thread. Do you throw it in front of you before you start, and all day the ball will be rolling ahead of you, and you'll be following behind winding the thread into another ball."

He obeyed the old woman, threw the ball down, and followed. All the day he was going uphill and down, across valleys and open places, keeping the ball in sight and winding the thread as he went, till evening, when he saw a hill in front, and a small light at the foot of it.

He went to the light and found a house, which he entered. There was no one inside but an old woman with teeth as long as a crutch.

"Oh! You are welcome to my house, king's son of Erin," said she. "You were with my sister last night; you are with me tonight. It's glad I am to see you."

She gave him meat and drink and a good bed to lie on.

When he rose next morning breakfast was there before him, and when he had eaten and was ready for the journey, the old woman gave him a ball of thread, saying, "You were with my younger sister the night before last, you were with me last night, and you'll be with my elder sister tonight. You must do what she tells you, or you'll lose your head. You must throw this ball before you, and follow the clew till evening."

He threw down the ball. It rolled on, showing the way up and down mountains and hills, across valleys and braes. All day he wound the ball. Unceasingly it went till nightfall, when he came to a light, found a little house, and went in.

Inside was an old woman, the eldest sister, who said, "You are welcome, and glad am I to see you, king's son."

She treated him as well as the other two had done. After he had eaten breakfast next morning, she said, "I know well the journey you are on. You have lost your head to the Giant of Loch Léin, and you are going to give yourself up. This giant has a great castle. Around the castle are seven hundred iron spikes, and on every spike of them but one is the head of a king, a queen, or a king's son. The seven hundredth spike is empty, and nothing can save your head from that spike if you don't take my advice.

"Here is a ball for you. Walk behind it till you come to a lake near the giant's castle. When you come to that lake at midday the ball will be unwound.

"The giant has three young daughters, and they come at noon every day of the year to bathe in the lake. You must watch them well, for each will have a lily on her breast. One a blue, another a white, and the third a yellow lily. You mustn't let your eyes off the one with the yellow lily. Watch her well: when she undresses to go into the water, see where she puts her clothes. When the three are out in the lake swimming, do you slip away with the clothes of Yellow Lily.

"When the sisters come out from bathing, and find that the one with the yellow lily has lost her clothes, the other two will laugh and make game of her. She will crouch down crying on the shore, with nothing to cover her, and say, '*How can I go home now, and everybody making sport of me? Whoever took my clothes, if he'll give them back to me, I'll save him from the danger he is in, if I have the power.*'"

The king's son followed the ball till nearly noon, when it stopped at a lake not far from the giant's castle. Then he hid behind a rock at the water's edge, and waited.

At midday the three sisters came to the lake, and leaving their clothes on the strand, went into the water. When all three were in the lake swimming and playing with great pleasure and sport, the king's son slipped out and took the clothes of the sister with the yellow lily.

After they had bathed in the lake to their hearts' content, the three sisters came out. When the two with the blue and the white lilies saw their sister on the shore and her clothes gone, they began to laugh and make sport of her.

Cowering and crouching down, she began to cry and lament, saying, "How can I go home now, with my own sisters laughing at me? If I stir from this, everybody will see me and make sport of me."

The sisters went home and left her there. When they were gone, and she was alone at the water crying and sobbing, all at once she came to herself and called out, "Whoever took my clothes, I'll forgive him if he brings them to me now, and I'll save him from the danger he is in if I can."

When he heard this, the king's son put the clothes out to her, and stayed behind till she told him to come forth.

She said, "I know well where you are going. My father, the Giant of Loch Léin, has a soft bed waiting for you: a deep tank of water for your death. But don't be uneasy. Go into the water, and wait till I come to save you. Be at that castle above before my father. When he comes home tonight and asks for you, take no meat from him, but go to rest in the tank when he tells you."

The giant's daughter left the king's son, who went his way to the castle alone at a fair and easy gait, for he had time enough on his hands and to spare.

When the Giant of Loch Léin came home that night, the first question he asked was, "Is the son of the king of Erin here?"

"I am," said the king's son.

"Come," said the giant, "and get your evening's meat."

"I'll take no meat now, for I don't need it," said the king's son.

"Well, come with me then, and I'll show you your bed."

He went, and the giant put the king's son into the deep tank of water to drown. Being tired himself from hunting all day over the mountains and hills of Erin, he went to sleep.

That minute his youngest daughter came, took the king's son out of the tank, placed plenty to eat and drink before him, and gave him a good bed to sleep on that night. She watched till she heard her father stirring before daybreak, then she roused the king's son and put him in the tank again.

Soon the giant came to the tank and called out, "Are you here, son of the king of Erin?"

"I am," said the king's son.

"Well, come out now. There is a great work for you today. I have a stable outside, in which I keep five hundred horses, and that stable has not been cleaned these seven hundred years. My great-grandmother when a girl lost a *bar an suan* somewhere in that stable, and never could find it. You must have that pin for me when I come home tonight. If you don't' your head will be on the seven hundredth spike tomorrow."

Two shovels were brought for the king's son to choose from to clean out the stable; an old and a new one. He chose the new shovel, and went to work.

For every shovelful he threw out, two came in. Soon the door of the stable was closed on him. When the stable door was closed, the giant's daughter called from outside: "How are you thriving now, king's son?"

"I'm not thriving at all. For as much as I throw out, twice as much comes in, and the door is closed against me."

"You must make a way for me to come in, and I'll help you," said she.

"How can I do that?"

However, she did it. The giant's daughter made her way into the stable, and wasn't long inside till the stable was cleared, and she saw the *bar an suan*.

"There is the pin over there in the corner," said she to the king's son, who put it in his bosom to give to the giant.

Now he was happy, and the giant's daughter had good meat and drink put before him.

When the giant himself came home, he asked, "How did you do your work today?"

"I did it well; I thought nothing of it."

"Did you find the *bar an suan?*"

"I did indeed. Here tis for you."

"Oh! Then," said the giant, "it is either the devil or my daughter that helped you to do that work, for I know you never did it alone."

"It's neither the devil nor your daughter, but my own strength that did the work," said the son of the king of Erin.

"You have done the work; now you must have your meat."

"I want no meat today. I am well satisfied as I am," said the king's son.

"Well," said the giant, "since you'll have no meat, you must go to sleep in the tank."

The king's son went into the tank. The giant himself was soon snoring, for he was tired from hunting over Erin all day.

The moment her father was away, Yellow Lily came, took the king's son out of the tank, gave him a good supper and bed, and watched till the giant was stirring before daybreak. Then she roused the king's son and put him in the tank.

"Are you alive in the tank?" asked the giant at daybreak.

"I am."

"You have a great work before you today. That stable you cleaned yesterday hasn't been thatched these seven hundred years. If you don't have it thatched for me when I come home tonight, with birds' feathers, and not two feathers of one color or kind, I'll have your head on the seven hundredth spike tomorrow. Here are two whistles. An old, and a new one. Take your choice of them to call the birds."

The king's son took the new whistle, and set out over the hills and valleys, whistling as he went. But no matter how he whistled, not a bird came near him. At last, tired and worn out with traveling and whistling, he sat down on a hillock and began to cry.

That moment Yellow Lily was at his side with a cloth, which she spread out, and there was a grand meal before him. He hadn't finished eating and drinking, before the stable was thatched with birds' feathers, and no two of them of one color or kind.

When he came home that evening the giant called out, "Have you the stable thatched for me tonight?"

"I have indeed," said the king's son. "And small trouble I had with it."

"If that's true, either the devil or my daughter helped you."

"It was my own strength, and not the devil or your daughter that helped me."

The king's son spent that night as he had the two nights before.

Next morning, when the giant found him alive in the tank, he said, "There is great work before you today, which you must do, or your head'll be on the spike tomorrow. Below here, under my castle, is a tree nine hundred feet high. There isn't a limb on that tree, from the roots up, except one small limb at the very top, where there is a crow's nest. The tree is covered with glass from the ground to the crow's nest. In the nest is one egg. You must have that egg before me here for my supper tonight, or I'll have your head on the seven hundredth spike tomorrow."

The giant went hunting, and the king's son went down to the tree, tried to shake it, but could not make it stir. Then he tried to climb, but no use, it was all slippery glass. Then he thought, "Sure I'm done for now; I must lose my head this time."

He stood there in sadness, when Yellow Lily came, and said, "How are you thriving in your work?"

"I can do nothing," said the king's son.

"Well, all that we have done up to this time is nothing to climbing this tree. But first of all let us sit down together and eat, and then we'll talk," said Yellow Lily. They sat down, she spread the cloth again, and they had a splendid feast. When the feast was over she took out a knife from her pocket and said, "Now you must kill me, strip the flesh from my bones, take all the bones apart, and use them as steps for climbing the tree. When you are climbing the tree, they will stick to the glass as if they had grown out of it. But when you are coming down, and have put your foot on each one, they will drop into your hand when you touch them. Be sure and stand on each bone, leave none untouched. If you do it will stay behind. Put all my flesh into this clean cloth by the side of the spring at the roots of the tree. When you come to the earth, arrange my bones together, put the flesh over them, sprinkle it with water from the spring, and I shall be alive and well before you. But don't forget a bone of me on the tree."

"How could I kill you!" cried the king's son, "after what you have done for me?"

"If you won't obey, you and I are done for. You must climb the tree or we are lost. And to climb the tree you must do as I say."

The king's son obeyed. He killed Yellow Lily, cut the flesh from her body, and unjointed the bones, as she had told him.

As he went up, the king's son put the bones of Yellow Lily's body against the side of the tree, using them as steps, till he came under the nest and stood on the last bone.

Then he took the crow's egg and coming down, put his foot on every bone, then took it with him, till he came to the last bone, which was so near the ground that he failed to touch it with his foot.

He now placed all the bones of Yellow Lily in order

again at the side of the spring, put the flesh on them, sprinkled it with water from the spring.

She rose up before him. "Didn't I tell you not to leave a bone of my body without stepping on it? Now I am lame for life! You left my little toe on the tree without touching it, and I have but nine toes."

When the giant came home that night, the first words he had were, "Have you the crow's egg for my supper?"

"I have," said the king's son.

"If you have, then either the devil or my daughter is helping you."

"It is my own strength that's helping me."

"Well, whoever it is, I must forgive you now, and your head is your own."

So the king's son was free to go his own road, and away he went, and never stopped till he came home to his own father and mother, who had a great welcome before him. And why not? For they thought he was dead.

When the son was at home a time, the king called up the old blind sage, and asked, "What must I do with my son now?"

"If you follow my advice," said the old blind sage, "you'll find a wife for him, and then he'll not go roaming away again, and leave you as he did before."

The king was pleased with the advice, and he sent a message to the king of Lochlin, known as Denmark today, to ask for his daughter in marriage. The king of Lochlin came with the daughter and a ship full of attendants, and there was to be a grand wedding at the castle of the king of Erin. Now, the king's son asked his father to invite the Giant of Loch Léin and Yellow Lily to the wedding. The king sent messages for them to come.

The day before the marriage there was a great feast at the castle. As the feast went on, and all were merry, the Giant of Loch Léin said, "I never was at a place like this but one man sang a song, a second told a story, and the third played a trick."

The king of Erin sang a song, the king of Lochlin told a story, and when the turn came to the giant, he asked Yellow Lily to take his place. She threw two grains of wheat in the air, and there came down on the table two pigeons. The cock pigeon pecked at the hen and pushed her off the table.

Then the hen called out to him in a human voice, "You wouldn't do that to me the day I cleaned the stable for you."

Next time Yellow Lily put two grains of wheat on the table. The cock ate the wheat, pecked the hen, and pushed her off the table to the floor.

The hen said, "You would not do that to me the day I thatched the stable for you with birds' feathers, and not two of one color or kind."

The third time Yellow Lily put two more grains of wheat on the table. The cock ate both, and pushed the hen off to the floor.

The hen called out, "You wouldn't do that to me the day you killed me, and took my bones to make steps up the glass tree, nine hundred feet high to get the crow's egg for the supper of the Giant of Loch Léin, and forget my little toe when you were coming down, and left me lame for life."

"Well," said the king's son to the guests at the feast. "When I was a little younger than I am now, I used to be everywhere in the world sporting and gaming. Once when I was away, I lost the key of a casket that I had. I had a new key made, and after it was brought to me I found the old one. Now, I'll leave it to anyone here to tell what am I to do. Which of the keys should I keep?"

"My advice to you," said the king of Lochlin, "is to keep the old key, for it fits the lock better, and you're more used to it."

The king's son stood up and said, "I thank you, king of Lochlin, for a wise advice and an honest word. This is my bride, the daughter of the Giant of Loch Léin. I'll have her, and no other woman. Your daughter is my father's guest, and no worse, but better, for having come to a wedding in Erin."

The king's son married Yellow Lily, daughter of the Giant of Loch Léin, the wedding lasted long, and all were happy.

13.

SHAKING-HEAD

THERE WAS once a king of a province in Erin who had an only son. The king was very careful of this son, and sent him to school for good instruction.

The other three kings of provinces in Erin had three sons at the same school and the three sent word by this one to his father, that if he didn't put his son to death they would put both father and son to death themselves.

When the young man came home with this word to his father and mother, they were grieved when they heard it. But the king's son said that he would go out into the world to seek his fortune, and settle the trouble in that way. So away he went, taking with him only five pounds in money for his support.

The young man traveled on till he came to a graveyard, where he saw four men fighting over a coffin. He went up to the four, and saw that two of them were trying to put the coffin down into a grave, and the other two were preventing them and keeping the coffin above ground.

When the king's son came near the men, he asked, "Why do you fight in such a place as this, and why do you keep the coffin above ground?"

Two of the men answered, "The body of our brother is

in this coffin, and these two men won't let us bury it."

The other two then said, "We have a debt of five pounds on the dead man, and we won't let his body be buried till the debt is paid."

The king's son said, "Do you let these men bury their brother, and I will pay what you ask."

The two let the brothers of the dead man bury him. The king's son paid the five pounds, and went away empty-handed. Except for the clothes on his back, he had no more than on the day he was born. After he had gone on his way awhile and the graveyard was out of sight he turned and saw a sprightly red-haired man hurrying after him.

When he came up, the stranger asked, "Don't you want a serving man?"

"I do not," answered the king's son. "I have nothing to support myself with, let alone a serving man."

"Never mind that," said the red-haired man. "I'll be with you wherever you go, whether you have anything or not."

"What is your name?" asked the king's son.

"Shaking-head," answered the red man.

When they had gone on a piece of the way together the king's son stopped and asked, "Where shall we be tonight?"

"We shall be in a giant's castle where there will be small welcome for us," said Shaking-head.

When evening came they found themselves in front of a castle. In they went and saw no one inside only a tall old hag. But they were not long in the place till they heard a loud, rushing noise outside, and a blow on the castle.

A giant came, and the first words he let out of his mouth were, "I'm glad to have an *Erinach* on my supper table to eat to-night." Turning to the two he asked, "What brought you here this evening; what do you want in my castle?"

"All the champions and heroes of Erin are going to take your property from you and destroy yourself. We have come to warn you, and there is nobody to save you from them but us," said Shaking-head.

When the giant heard these words he changed his treatment entirely. He gave the king's son and Shaking-head a hearty welcome and a kindly greeting. When he understood the news they brought, he washed them with the tears of his eyes, dried them with kisses, and gave them a good supper and a soft bed that night.

Next morning the giant was up at an early hour, and he went to the bedside of each man and told him to rise and have breakfast. Shaking-head asked his reward of the giant for telling him of the champions of Erin and the danger he was in.

"Well," said the giant, "there's a pot of gold over there under my bed. Take as much out of it as ever you wish, and welcome."

"It isn't gold I want for my service," said Shaking-head. "You have a gift which suits me better."

"What gift is that?" asked the giant.

"The light black steed in your stable."

"That's a gift I won't give you. For when anyone comes to trouble or attack me, all I have to do is to throw my leg over that steed, and away he carries me out of sight of every enemy."

"Well," said Shaking-head, "if you don't give me that steed I'll bring all the kingdom of Erin against you, and you'll be destroyed with all you have."

The giant stopped a moment, and said, "I believe you'd do that thing, so you may take the steed."

Shaking-head took the steed of the giant, gave him to the king's son, and away they went.

At sunset Shaking-head said, "We are near the castle of another giant; the next brother to the one who entertained us last night. He hasn't much welcome for us either, but he will treat us well when he is threatened."

The second giant was going to eat the king's son for supper, but when Shaking-head told him about the forces of Erin he changed his manner and entertained them well.

Next morning after breakfast, Shaking-head said, "You must give me a present for my services in warning you."

"There is a pot of gold under my bed," said the giant. "Take all you want of it."

"I don't want your gold," said Shaking-head. "But you have a gift which suits me well."

"What is that?" asked the giant.

"The two-handed black sword that never fails a blow."

"You won't get that gift from me," said the giant. "And I can't spare it. For if a whole army were to come against me, as soon as I'd have my two hands on the hilt of that sword, I'd let no man near me without sweeping the head off him."

"Well," said Shaking-head, "I have been keeping back your enemies this long time. But I'll let them at you now, and I'll raise up more. I'll put the whole kingdom of Erin against you."

The giant stopped a moment, and said, "I believe you'd do that if it served you." So he took the sword off his belt and handed it to his guest.

Shaking-head gave it to the king's son, who mounted his steed, and they both went away. When they had gone some distance from the giant's castle, Shaking-head said to the king's son, "Where shall we be tonight? You have more knowledge than I."

"Indeed then, I have not," said the king's son. "I have no knowledge at all of where we are going. It is you who have the knowledge."

"Well," said Shaking-head, "we'll be at the third and youngest giant's castle tonight. At first he'll treat us far worse and more harshly, but still we'll take this night's lodging of him, and a good gift in the morning."

Soon after sunset they came to the castle, where they met the worst reception and the harshest they had found on the road. The giant was going to eat them both for supper, but when Shaking-head told him of the champions of Erin, he became as kind as his two brothers, and gave good entertainment to both.

Next morning after breakfast, Shaking-head asked for a present in return for his services.

"Do you see the pot of gold in the corner there under my bed? Take all you want and welcome," said the giant.

"It's not gold I want," said Shaking-head, "but the cloak of darkness."

"Oh," said the giant. "You'll not get that cloak of me, for I want it myself. If any man were to come against me, all I'd have to do would be to put that cloak on my shoulders and no one in the world could see me, or know where I'd be."

"Well," said Shaking-head, "it's long enough that I am keeping your enemies away. If you don't give me that cloak now I'll raise all the kingdom of Erin and still more forces to destroy you, and it's not long you'll last after they come."

The giant thought a moment, and then said, "I believe you'd do what you say. There's the black cloak hanging on the wall before you. Take it."

Shaking-head took the cloak, and the two went away together; the king's son riding on the light black steed and having the double-handed sword at his back. When out of sight of the giant, Shaking-head put on the cloak, and wasn't to be seen, and no other man could have been seen in his place.

The king's son looked around, and began to call and search for his man; he was lonely without him and grieved not to see him. Shaking-head, glad to see the affection of the king's son, took off the cloak and was at his side again.

"Where are we going now?" asked the king's son.

"We are going on a long journey to *Ri Chuil an Or*, the King Behind the Gold, to ask his daughter of him."

The two travelled on, till they came to the castle of King Behind the Gold. Then Shaking-head said, "Go in you, and ask his daughter of the king, and I'll stay here outside with the cloak on me."

So he went in and spoke to the king, and the answer he got was this: "I am willing to give you my daughter, but you won't get her unless you do what she will ask of you. And I must tell you now that three hundred kings' sons, lacking one, have come to ask for my daughter, and in the garden behind my castle are three hundred iron spikes. Every spike of them but one is covered with the head of a king's son who couldn't do what my daughter wanted of him. I'm greatly in dread that your own head will be put on the one spike that is left uncovered."

"Well," said the king's son, "I'll do my best to keep my head where it is at present."

"Stay here in my castle," said the king, "and you'll have good entertainment till we know can you do what will be asked of you."

At night when the king's son was going to bed, the princess gave him a thimble, and said, "Have this for me in the morning."

He put the thimble on his finger. She thought it could be easily taken away, if he would sleep. So she came to him in the night, with a drink, and said, "I give you this in hopes I'll gain more drink by you."

He swallowed the liquor, and the princess went away with the empty cup. Then the king's son put the thimble in his mouth between his cheek and his teeth for safe keeping, and was soon asleep.

When the princess came to her own chamber, she struck her maid with a *slat an draoichta*, a rod of enchantment, and turned her into a rat. Then she made such music of fifes and trumpets to sound throughout the castle, that every soul in it fell asleep. That minute, she sent the rat to where the king's son was sleeping. The rat put her tail into the nostrils of the young man, tickled his nose so that he sneezed and blew the thimble out of his mouth. The rat caught it and ran away to the princess, who struck her with the rod of enchantment and turned her into a maid again.

The princess and the maid set out for the eastern world, taking the thimble with them. Shaking-head, who was watching with his cloak on, unseen by all, followed at their heels. In the eastern world, at the seaside was a rock. The princess tapped it with her finger, and the rock opened. There was a great house inside, and in the house a giant.

The princess greeted him and gave him the thimble, saying, "You're to keep this so no man can get it."

"Oh," said the giant, taking the thimble and throwing it aside. "You need have no fear; no man can find me in this place."

Shaking-head caught the thimble from the ground and put it in his pocket. When she had finished conversation with the giant, the princess kissed him, and hurried away. Shaking-head followed her step for step, till they came at break of day to the castle of King Behind the Gold.

Shaking-head went to the king's son and asked, "Was anything given you to keep last night?"

"Yes, before I came to this chamber the princess gave me her thimble, and told me to have it for her in the morning."

"Have you it now?" asked Shaking-head.

"It is not in my mouth where I put it last night. It is not in the bed. I'm afraid my head is lost."

"Look at this," said Shaking-head, taking the thimble out of his pocket and giving it to him. "The whole kingdom is moving today to see your death. All the people have heard that you are here asking for the princess, and they think your head'll be put on the last spike in the garden, with the heads of the other kings' sons. Rise up now, mount your light black steed, ride to the summer house of the princess and her father, and give her the thimble."

The king's son did as Shaking-head told him. When he gave up the thimble, the king said, "You have won one third of my daughter."

But the princess was bitterly angry and vexed to the heart, that any man on earth should know that she had dealings with the giant. She cared more for that than anything else.

When the second day had passed, and the king's son was going to bed, the princess gave him a comb to keep, and said, "If you don't have this for me in the morning, your head will be put on the spike that's left in my father's garden."

The king's son took the comb with him, wrapped it in a handkerchief, and tied it to his head. In the night the princess came with a draught which she gave him, and soon he was asleep. Going back to her own chamber, she struck the maid with her rod of enchantment, and made a great yellow cat of her. Then she caused such music of fifes and trumpets to sound throughout the castle that every soul was in a deep sleep before the music was over, and that moment she sent the cat to the chamber of the king's son. The cat worked the handkerchief off his head, took out the comb and ran with it to the princess, who turned her into a maid again.

The two set out for the eastern world straightway. Shaking-head followed them in his cloak of darkness till they came to the house of the giant in the great rock at the end of the road, at the sea. The princess gave the giant the comb.

"The thimble that I gave you to keep last night was taken from you. The king's son in Erin brought it back to me this morning, and has done one third of the work of winning me. I didn't expect you'd serve me in this way."

When the giant heard this, he was raging, and threw the comb into the sea behind him. Then with Druidic spells he raised thunder and lightning and wind. The sea was roaring with storm and rain, but the comb had not touched the water when Shaking-head caught it.

When her talk was over the princess gave the giant a kiss, and home she went with the maid. Shaking-head followed them step by step.

In the morning Shaking-head went to the king's son, roused him, and asked, "What was your task last night?"

"The princess gave me a comb to have for her this morning," answered the king's son.

"Where is it now?"

"Here on my head." He put up his hand to get it, but the comb was gone. "I'm done for now. My head will be on the last spike today unless I have the comb for the princess."

"Here it is for you." Shaking-head took the comb out of his pocket. "And now," said he, "the whole kingdom is coming to this castle today to see your head put on the last spike in the garden of King Behind the Gold. For all men think the same will happen to you that has happened to every king's son before you. Go up on your steed and ride to the summer house where the king and his daughter are sitting, and give her the comb."

The king's son did as Shaking-head bade him. When he saw the comb the king said, "Now you have my daughter two-thirds won."

But her face went from the princess entirely. She was so vexed that any man should know of her dealings with the giant.

The third night when he was going to bed the princess said to the king's son, "If you will not have at my father's castle tomorrow morning, the head I will kiss tonight, you'll die tomorrow, and your own head will be put on the last spike in my father's garden."

Later in the night she came to the bedside of the king's son with a draught. Which he drank, and before she was back in her chamber, he slept. Then she made such music all over the castle that not a soul was awake when the music had ceased. That moment she hurried away with her maid to the eastern world with Shaking-head following her in his cloak of darkness. This time he carried with him the two-handed sword that never failed a blow.

When she came to the rock in the eastern world and entered the house of the giant, the princess said, "You let my two gifts go with the son of the king in Erin, and he'll have me won tomorrow if he'll have your head at my father's castle in the morning."

"Never fear," said the giant. "There is nothing in the world to take the head off me but the double-handed sword of darkness that never fails a blow, and that sword belongs to my brother in the western world."

The princess gave the giant a kiss at parting. As she hurried away with her maid the giant turned to look at her. His head was covered with an iron cap, but as he looked he laid bare a thin strip of his neck.

Shaking-head was there near him, and said in his mind, "Your brother's sword has never been so close to your neck before." With one blow he swept the head off him. Then began the greatest struggle that Shaking-head ever had; to keep the head from the body of the giant. The head fought to put itself on again, and never stopped till the body was dead. Then it fell to the ground. Shaking-head seized, but couldn't stir the head, couldn't move it from its place. Then he searched all around it and found a *bar an suan* near the ear. When he took the pin away he had no trouble in carrying the head. He made no delay but came to the castle at daybreak, and threw the head to a herd of pigs that belonged to the king.

Then he went to the king's son. "What happened to you last night?"

"The princess came to me, and said that if I wouldn't bring to her father's castle this morning the head she was to kiss last night, my own head would be on the last spike today."

"Come out with me now to the pigs," said Shaking-head. The two went out, and Shaking-head said, "Go in among the pigs, and take the head with you to the king. A strange head it is to put before a king."

So the king's son went on his steed to the summer house, and gave the head to the king and his daughter.

Turning to the princess, he said, "This is the head you kissed last night, and it's not a nice looking head, either."

"You have my daughter won now entirely," said the king, "and she is yours. And do you take that head to the great dark hole that is out there on one side of my castle grounds, and throw it down."

The king's son mounted his steed, and rode off with the head till he came to the hole going deep into the earth. When he let down the head it went to the bottom with such a roaring and such a noise that every mare and cow and every beast in the whole kingdom cast its young, such was the terror that was caused by the noise of the head in going to the bottom of the hole.

When the head was put away the king's son went back to the castle, and married the daughter of King Behind the Gold. The wedding lasted nine days and nights, and the last night was better than the first.

When the wedding was over Shaking-head went to the king and said, "You have provided no fortune for your daughter, and it is but right that you should remember her."

"I have plenty of gold and silver to give her," said the king.

"It isn't gold and silver that your son-in-law wants, but men to stand against his enemies, when they come on him."

"I have more treasures than men," said King Behind the Gold. "But I won't see my daughter conquered for want of an army."

They were satisfied with the king's word, and next day took the road to Erin, and kept on their way till they came opposite the graveyard.

There Shaking-head said to the king's son, "You are no good. You have never told me a story since the first day I saw you."

"I have but one story to tell you, except what happened since we met."

"Well, tell me what happened before we met."

"I was passing this place before I saw you," said the king's son, "and four men were fighting over a coffin. I spoke to them, and two of them said they were burying the body of their brother, which was in the coffin. The others said the dead man owed them five pounds, and they wouldn't let the coffin into the ground until they got the money. I paid five pounds and the body was buried."

"It was my body was in the coffin," said Shaking-head. "I came back into this world to do you a good turn. And now I am going, and you'll never see me again unless trouble is on you."

Shaking-head disappeared, and the king's son went home. He wasn't with his father long till the other three kings' sons heard he had come back to Erin with the daughter of King Behind the Gold.

They sent word. "We'll take the head off you now, and put an end to your father and yourself."

The king's son went out to walk alone, and as he was lamenting the fate he had brought on his father, who should come along to meet him but Shaking-head.

"What trouble is on you now?" asked he.

"Three kings' sons are coming with their fleets and armies to destroy my father and myself, and what can we do with our one fleet and one army?"

"Well," said Shaking-head. "I'll settle that for you without delay." He sent a message straight to King Behind the Gold, who gave a fleet and an army. They came to Erin so quickly that they were at the castle before the forces of the three kings' sons. And when the three came the battle began on sea and land at both sides of the castle.

The three fleets of the three kings' sons were sunk, their armies destroyed, and the three heads taken off themselves. When the battle was over and the country safe, the king resigned the castle and power to his son, and the son of a king in a province became king over all the land of Erin.

14.

CONALL YELLOWCLAW

CONALL YELLOWCLAW was a sturdy tenant in Erin, and had three sons. There was at that time a king over every fifth of Erin. It fell out for the children of the king that was near Conall, that they themselves and the children of Conall came to blows. The children of Conall got the upper hand, and they killed the king's big son.

The king sent a message for Conall, and he said to him, "Oh, Conall! What made your sons go to spring on my sons till my big son was killed by your children? But I see that though I follow you revengefully, I shall not be much better for it, and I will now set a thing before you. If you will do it, I will not follow you with revenge. If you and your sons will get me the brown horse of the king of Lochlann, you shall get the souls of your sons."

"Why," said Conall, "should not I do the pleasure of the king, though there should be no souls of my sons in dread at all. Hard is the matter you require of me, but I will lose my own life, and the life of my sons, or else I will do the pleasure of the king."

After these words he left the king, and went home. When he got home he was under much trouble and perplexity. When he went to lie down he told his wife the thing the king had set before him. His wife took much sorrow that he was obliged to part from herself, while she knew not if she should see him more.

"Oh, Conall," said she. "Why didst not thou let the king do his own pleasure to thy sons, rather than be going now, while I know not if ever I shall see thee more?"

When he rose on the morrow, he set himself and his three sons in order, and they took their journey towards Lochlann. They made no stop but tore through ocean till they reached it. When they arrived at Lochlann they did not know what they should do.

Said the old man to his sons, "Stop ye, and we will seek out the house of the king's miller."

When they went into the house of the king's miller, the man asked them to stop there for the night. Conall told the miller that his own children and the children of his king had fallen out, that his children had killed the king's son, and there was nothing that would please the king but that he should get the brown horse of the king of Lochlann.

"If you will do me a kindness, and will put me in a way to get him, for certain I will pay ye for it."

"The thing is silly that you are come to seek," said the miller. "For the king has laid his mind on him so greatly that you will not get him in any way unless you steal him. But if you can make out a way, I will keep it secret."

"This is what I am thinking," said Conal. "Since you are working every day for the king, you and your gillies could put myself and my sons into five sacks of bran."

"The plan that has come into your head is not bad," said the miller. He spoke to his gillies, and he said to them to do this, and they put them in five sacks.

The king's gillies came to seek the bran, and they took the five sacks with them, and they emptied them before the horses. The servants locked the door, and they went away.

When they rose to lay hand on the brown horse, said

Conall, "You shall not do that. It is hard to get out of this. Let us make for ourselves five hiding holes, so that if they hear us we may go and hide."

They made the holes, and then they laid hands on the horse. The horse was pretty well unbroken, and he set to making a terrible noise through the stable.

The king heard the noise. "It must be my brown horse," said he to his gillies. "Find out what is wrong with him."

The servants went out, and when Conall and his sons saw them coming they went into the hiding holes. The servants looked amongst the horses, and they did not find anything wrong. They returned and told this to the king, and the king said that if nothing was wrong they should go to their places of rest.

When the gillies had time to be gone, Conall and his sons laid their hands again on the horse. If the noise was great that he made before, the noise he made now was seven times greater. The king sent a message for his gillies again, and said for certain there was something troubling the brown horse. "Go and look well about him."

The servants went out, and Conall and his sons went to their hiding holes. The servants rummaged well, and did not find a thing. They returned and they told this.

"That is marvelous for me," said the king. "Go you to lie down again, and if I notice it again I will go out myself."

When Conall and his sons perceived that the gillies were gone, they laid hands again on the horse. One of them caught him, and if the noise that the horse made on the two former times was great, he made more this time.

"Be this from me," said the king. "It must be that someone is troubling my brown horse."

He sounded the bell hastily, and when his waiting-man came to him, he told him to let the stable gillies know that something was wrong with the horse. The gillies came, and the king went with them. When Conall and his sons perceived the company coming they went to the hiding holes.

The king was a wary man, and he saw where the horses were making a noise. "Be wary," he said. "There are men within the stable. Let us get at them somehow."

The king followed the tracks of the men, and he found them. Everyone knew Conall, for he was a valued tenant of the king of Erin. When the king brought them up out of the holes he said, "Oh, Conall, is it you that are here?"

"I am, oh King, without question, and necessity made me come. I am under thy pardon, and under thine honor, and under thy grace." He told how it happened to him, and that he had to get the brown horse for the king of Erin, or that his sons were to be put to death. "I knew that I should not get him by asking, and I was going to steal him."

"Yes, Conall, it is well enough, but come in," said the king. He desired his lookout men to set a watch on the sons of Conall, and to give them meat. And a double watch was set that night on the sons of Conall.

"Now, Conall," said the king. "Were you ever in a harder place than to be seeing your lot of sons hanged tomorrow? But you set it to my goodness and to my grace, and say that it was necessity brought it on you, so I must not hang you. Tell me any case in which you were as hard as this, and if you tell that, you shall get the soul of your youngest son."

"I will tell a case as hard in which I was," said Conall. "I was once a young lad and my father had much land. He had parks of year-old cows, and one of them had just calved, and my father told me to bring her home. I found the cow, and took her with us. There fell a shower of snow. We went into the herd's *bothy*, and we took the cow and the calf in with us. We were letting the shower pass from us. Who should come in but one cat and ten, and one great one-eyed fox-colored cat as head bard over them? When they came in, in very deed I myself had no liking for their company. 'Strike up with you,' said the head bard, 'why should we be still? Sing a *cronan* to Conall Yellowclaw.' ' was amazed that my name was known to the cats themselves. When they had sung the *cronan*, said the head bard, 'Now, O Conall, pay the reward of the *cronan* that the cats have sung to thee.' 'Well then,' said I myself, 'I have no reward whatsoever for you, unless you should go down and take that calf.' No sooner said I the word than the two cats and ten went down to attack the calf, and in very deed, he did not last them long. 'Play up with you, why should you be silent? Make a *cronan* to Conall Yellowclaw,' said the head bard. Certainly I had no liking at all for the *cronan*, but up came the one cat and ten, and if they did not sing me a *cronan* then and there! 'Pay them now their reward,' said the great fox-colored cat. 'I am tired myself of yourselves and your rewards,' said I. 'I have no reward for you unless you take that cow down there.' They betook themselves to the cow, and indeed she did not last them long.

"'Why will you be silent? Go up and sing a *cronan* to Conall Yellowclaw,' said the head bard. And surely, oh king, I had no care for them or for their *cronan*, for I began to see that they were not good comrades. When they had sung me the *cronan* they betook themselves down where the head bard was. 'Pay now their reward, said the head bard. For sure, oh king, I had no reward for them, and I said to them, 'I have no reward for you.' And surely, oh king, there was caterwauling between them. So I leapt out at a turf window that was at the back of the house. I took myself off as hard as I might into the wood. I was swift enough and strong at that time, and when I felt the rustling *toirm* of the cats after me I climbed into as high a tree as I saw in the place. One that was close in the top and I hid myself as well as I might.

The cats began to search for me through the wood, and they could not find me. When they were tired, each one said to the other that they would turn back. 'But,' said the one-eyed fox-colored cat that was commander-in-chief over them, 'you saw him not with your two eyes, and though I have but one eye, there's the rascal up in the tree.' Then he had said that, one of them went up in the tree, and as he was coming where I was, I drew a weapon that I had and I killed him. 'I must not be losing my company thus,' said the one-eyed one. 'Gather round the root of the tree and dig about it, and let down that villain to earth.' On this they gathered about the tree, and they dug about the root, and the first branching root that they cut, she gave a shiver to fall, and I myself gave a shout, and it was not to be wondered at.

"There was in the neighborhood of the wood a priest, and he had ten men with him delving, and he said, 'That is a shout of a man in extremity and I must not be without replying to it.' And the wisest of the men said, 'Let it alone till we hear it again.' The cats began again digging wildly, and they broke the next root. I myself gave the next shout, and in very deed it was not a weak one. 'Certainly,' said the priest, 'it is a man in extremity; let us move.' They set themselves in order for moving. And the cats arose on the tree, and they broke the third root, and the tree fell on her elbow. Then I gave the third shout. The stalwart men hastened, and when they saw how the cats served the tree, they began at them with the spades, and they themselves and the cats began at each other, till the cats ran away. And surely, oh king, I did not move till I saw the last one of them off. And then I came home. And there's the hardest case in which I ever was, and it seems to me that tearing by the cats were harder than hanging tomorrow by the king of Lochlann."

"Och! Conall," said the king, "you are full of words. You have freed the soul of your son with your tale, and if you tell me a harder case than that you will get your second youngest son, and then you will have two sons."

"Well then," said Conall. "On condition that thou dost that, I will tell thee how I was once in a harder case than to be in thy power in prison tonight."

"Let's hear."

"I was then quite a young lad, and I went out hunting. My father's land was beside the sea, and it was rough with rocks, caves, and rifts. When I was going on the top of the shore, I saw as if there were a smoke coming up between two rocks, and I began to look what might be the meaning of the smoke coming up there. When I was looking, what should I do but fall, and the place was so full of heather, that neither bone nor skin was broken. I knew not how I should get out of this. I was not looking before me, but I kept looking overhead the way I came, and thinking that the day would never come that I could get up there. It was terrible for me to be there till I should die. I heard a great clattering coming, and what was there but a great giant and two dozen of goats with him, and a buck at their head. And when the giant had tied the goats, he came up and he said to me, 'Hail, oh Conall, it's long since my knife has been rusting in my pouch waiting for thy tender flesh.' 'Och!' said I, 'it's not much you will be bettered by me. Though you should tear me asunder, I will make but one meal for you. But I see that you are one-eyed. I am a good leech, and I will give you the sight of the other eye.' The giant went and he drew the great caldron on the site of the fire. I myself was telling him how he should heat the water, so that I should give its sight to the other eye. I got heather and I made a rubber of it, and I set him upright in the caldron. I began at the eye that was well, pretending to him that I would give its sight to the other one, till I left them as bad as each other, and surely it was easier to spoil the one that was well than to give sight to the other.

"When he saw that he could not see a glimpse, and when I myself said to him that I would get out in spite of him, he gave a spring out of the water. He stood in the mouth of the cave and said that he would have revenge for the sight of his eye. I had but to stay there crouched the length of the night, holding in my breath in such a way that he might not find out where I was.

"When he felt the birds calling in the morning, and knew that the day was, he said, 'Art thou sleeping? Awake and let out my lot of goats.' I killed the buck. He cried, 'I do believe that thou art killing my buck.'

"I am not,' said I, 'but the ropes are so tight that I take long to loose them.' I let out one of the goats, and there he was caressing her, and he said to her, 'There thou art thou shaggy, hairy white goat. Thou seest me, but I see thee not.' I kept letting them out by the way of one and one, as I flayed the buck, and before the last one was out I had him flayed bag-wise. Then I went and I put my legs in place of his legs, and my hands in place of his forelegs, and my head in place of his head, and the horns on top of my head, so that the brute might think that it was the buck. I went out. When I was going out the giant laid his hand on me, and he said, 'There thou art, thou pretty buck; thou seest me, but I see thee not.' Then I myself got out, and I saw the world about me, surely, oh, king! Joy was on me. When I was out and had shaken the skin off me, I said to the brute, 'I am out now in spite of you.'

"'Aha!' said he, 'hast thou done this to me. Since thou wert so stalwart that thou hast got out, I will give thee a ring that I have here. Keep the ring, and it will do thee good.'

"I will not take the ring from you,' said I, 'but throw it, and I will take it with me.' He threw the ring on the flat ground, I went myself and I lifted the ring, and I put it on my finger. When he said me then, 'Is the ring fitting thee?' I said to him, 'It is.' Then he said, 'Where art thou, ring?' And the ring answered, 'I am here.' The brute went and went towards where the ring was speaking, and now I saw that I was in a harder case than ever I was. I drew a dirk. I cut the finger from off me, and I threw it from me as far as I could out on the loch, and there was a great depth in the place. He shouted, 'Where art thou, ring?' And the ring said, 'I am here,' though it was on the bed of ocean. He gave a spring after the ring, and out he went in the sea. And I was as pleased then when I saw him drowning, as though you should grant my own life and the life of my two sons with me, and not lay any more trouble on me.

"When the giant was drowned I went in, and I took with me all he had of gold and silver, and I went home, and surely great joy was on my people when I arrived. And as a sign now look, the finger is off me."

"Yes, indeed, Conall, you are wordy and wise," said the king. "I see the finger is off you. You have freed your two sons, but tell me a case in which you ever were that is harder than to be looking on your son being hanged tomorrow, and you shall get the soul of your eldest son."

"Then went my father," said Conall, "and he got me a wife, and I was married. I went to hunt. I was going beside the sea, and I saw an island over in the midst of the loch, and I came there where a boat was with a rope before her, and a rope behind her, and many precious things within her. I looked myself on the boat to see how I might get part of them. I put in the one foot, and the other foot was on the ground, and when I raised my head what was it but the boat over in the middle of the loch, and she never stopped till she reached the island. When I went out of the boat the boat returned where she was before. I did not know now what I should do. The place was without meat or clothing, without the appearance of a house on it. I came out on the top of a hill. Then I came to a glen. I saw in it, at the bottom of a hollow, a woman with a child, and the child was naked on her knee, and she had a knife in her hand. She tried to put the knife to the throat of the babe, and the babe began to laugh in her face, and she began to cry, and she threw the knife behind her. I thought to myself that I was near my foe and far from my friends, and I called to the woman, 'What are you doing here?' And she said to me, 'What brought you here?' I told her myself word upon word how I came. 'Well then,' said she, 'it was so I came also.' She showed me to the place where I should come in where she was. I went in, and I said to her, 'What was the matter that you were putting the knife on the neck of the child?'

"'It is that he must be cooked for the giant who is here, or else no more of my world will be before me.' Just then we could be hearing the footsteps of the giant, 'What shall I do? What shall I do?' cried the woman. I went to the caldron, and by luck it was not hot, so in it I got just as the brute came in. 'Hast thou boiled that youngster for me?' he cried. 'He's not done yet,' said she, and I cried out from the caldron, 'Mammy, mammy! It's boiling I am.' Then the giant laughed out, '*Hai, haw, hogaraich!*' and heaped on wood under the caldron.

"Now I was sure I would scald before I could get out of that. As fortune favored me, the brute slept beside the caldron. There I was scalded by the bottom of the caldron. When she perceived that he was asleep, she set her mouth quietly to the hole that was in the lid, and she said to me 'Are you alive?' I said I was. I put up my head, and the hole in the lid was so large, that my head went through easily. Everything was coming easily with me till I began to bring up my hips. I left the skin of my hips behind me, but I came out. When I got out of the caldron I knew not what to do. She said to me that there was no weapon that would kill him but his own weapon. I began to draw his spear and every breath that he drew I thought I would be down his throat, and when his breath came out I was back again just as far. But with every ill that befell me I got the spear loosed from him. Then I was as one under a bundle of straw in a great wind for I could not manage the spear. And it was fearful to look on the brute, who had but one eye in the midst of his face, and it was not agreeable for the like of me to attack him. I drew the dart as best I could, and I set it in his eye. When he felt this he gave his head a lift, and he struck the other end of the dart on the top of the cave, and it went through to the back of his head. And he fell cold dead where he was; and you may be sure, oh king, that joy was on me. I myself and the woman went out on clear ground, and we passed the night there. I went and got the boat with which I came, and she was no way lightened, and took the woman and the child over on dry land. Then I returned home."

The king of Lochlann's mother was putting on a fire at this time, and listening to Conall telling the tale about the child.

"Is it you," asked she, "that were there?"

"Well, then," said he. "'Twas I."

"Och! Och!" cried she. "'Twas I that was there and the king is the child whose life you saved. It is to you that life thanks should be given." Then they took great joy.

The king said, "Oh, Conall, you came through great hardships. And now the brown horse is yours, and his sack full of the most precious things that are in my treasury.'"

They lay down that night, and if it was early that Conall rose, it was earlier than that that the queen was on foot making ready. He got the brown horse and his sack full of gold and silver and stones of great price, and then Conall and his three sons went away, and they returned home to the Erin realm of gladness. He left the gold and silver in his house, and he went with the horse to the king. They were good friends evermore. He returned home to his wife, and they set in order a feast; and that was a feast if ever there was one, oh son and brother.

15.

THE CHILD'S DREAM

THE ISLAND of Innis-Sark, known today as Shark Island, was a holy and peaceful place in old times. So quiet that pigeons used to come and build in a great cave by the sea, and no one disturbed them. And the holy saints of God had a monastery there, to which many people resorted from the mainland, for the prayers of the monks were powerful against sickness or evil, or the malice of an enemy.

Amongst others, there came a great and noble prince out of Munster, with his wife and children and their nurse. They were so pleased with the island that they remained a year or more, for the prince loved fishing and often brought his wife along with him.

One day, while they were both away, the eldest child, a beautiful boy of ten years old, begged his nurse to let him go amid see the pigeons' cave, but she refused.

"Your father would be angry," she cried, "if you went without leave. Wait till he comes home, and see if he will allow you."

So when the prince returned, the boy told him how he longed to see the cave, and the father promised to bring him next day.

The morning was beautiful and the wind fair when they set off. But the child soon fell asleep in the boat and never wakened all the time his father was fishing. The sleep, however, was troubled, and many a time he started and cried aloud. So the prince thought it better to turn the boat and land, and then the boy awoke.

After dinner the father called for the child. "Tell me, now," he said, "why was your sleep troubled, so that you cried out bitterly in your dream?"

"I dreamed," said the boy, "that I stood upon a high rock, and at the bottom flowed the sea, but the waves made no noise. As I looked down I saw fields and trees and beautiful flowers and bright birds in the branches, and I longed to go down and pluck the flowers. Then I heard a voice, saying, 'Blessed are the souls that come here, for this is heaven.'

'And in an instant I thought I was in the midst of the meadows amongst the birds and the flowers. A lovely lady, bright as an angel, came up to me, and said, 'What brings you here, dear child? For none but the dead come here.'

'Then she left me, and I wept for her going, when suddenly all the sky grew black, and a great troop of wild wolves came round me, howling and opening their mouths wide as if to devour me. I screamed and tried to run, but I could not move. The wolves came closer, and I fell down like one dead with fright when, just then, the beautiful lady came again, and took my hand and kissed me.

"'Fear not,' 'he said, 'take these flowers, they come from heaven. And I will bring you to the meadow where they grow.'

'And she lifted me up into the air, but I know nothing more, for then the boat stopped and you lifted me on shore. My beautiful flowers must have fallen from my hands, for I never saw them more. And this is all my dream. But I would like to have my flowers again, for the lady told me they had the secret that would bring me to heaven."

The prince thought no more of the child's dream and went off to fish next day as usual, leaving the boy in the care of his nurse. And again the child begged and prayed her so earnestly to bring him to the pigeons' cave, that at last she consented. But told him he must not go a step by himself, and she would bring two of the boys of the island to take care of him.

So they set off, the child and his little sister with the nurse. The boy gathered wild flowers for his sister, and ran down to the edge of the cave where the cormorants were swimming, but there was no danger, for the two young islanders were minding him.

So the nurse was content, and being weary she fell asleep. And the little sister lay down beside her, and fell asleep likewise.

Then the boy called to his companions, the two young islanders, and told them he must catch the cormorants. So away they ran, down the path to the sea, hand in hand, and laughing as they went. Just then a piece of rock loosened and fell beside them. Trying to avoid it they slipped over the edge of the narrow path down a steep place, where there was nothing to hold on by except a large bush, in the middle of the way. They got hold of this, and thought they were now quite safe, but the bush was not strong enough to bear their weight, and it was torn up by the roots. And all three fell straight down into the sea and were drowned.

Now, at the sound of the great cry that came up from the waves, the nurse awoke, but saw no one. Then she woke up the little sister.

"It is late!" she cried. "They must have gone home. We have slept too long; it is already evening. Let us hasten and overtake them, before the prince is back from the fishing."

But when they reached home the prince stood in the doorway. And he was very pale, and weeping.

"Where is my brother?" cried the little girl.

"You will never see your brother more," answered the prince.

And from that day he never went fishing any more, but grew silent and thoughtful, and was never seen to smile. And in a short time he and his family quitted the island, never to return.

But the nurse remained. And some say she became a saint, for she was always seen praying and weeping by the entrance to the great sea cave. And one day, when they came to look for her, she lay dead on the rocks. And in her hand she held some beautiful strange flowers freshly gathered, with the dew on them. And no one knew how the flowers came into her dead hand. Only some fishermen told the story of how the night before they had seen a bright faery child seated on the rocks singing, and he had a red sash tied round his waist and a golden circlet binding his long yellow hair. And they all knew that he was the prince's son, who had been drowned in that spot just a twelvemonth before. And the people believe that he had brought the flowers from the spirit land to the woman, and given them to her as a death sign, and a blessed token from God that her soul would be taken to heaven.

16.

FAIR, BROWN AND TREMBLING

KING AEDH CURUCHA lived in Tir Conal, and he had three daughters, whose names were Fair, Brown, and Trembling.

Fair and Brown had new dresses, and went to church every Sunday. Trembling was kept at home to do the cooking and work. They would not let her go out of the house at all, for she was more beautiful than the other two, and they were in dread she might marry before themselves.

They carried on in this way for seven years. At the end of seven years the son of the king of Omanya, the ancient Emania in Ulster, fell in love with the eldest sister.

One Sunday morning, after the other two had gone to church, the old henwife came into the kitchen to Trembling, and said, "It's at church you ought to be this day, instead of working here at home."

"How could I go?" answered Trembling. "I have no clothes good enough to wear at church and if my sisters were to see me there, they'd kill me for going out of the house."

"I'll give you," said the henwife, "a finer dress than either of them has ever seen. And now tell me what dress will you have?"

"I'll have," said Trembling, "a dress as white as snow,

and green shoes for my feet."

The henwife put on the cloak of darkness, clipped a piece from the old clothes the young woman had on, and asked for the whitest robes in the world and the most beautiful that could be found, and a pair of green shoes.

That moment she had the robe and the shoes, and she brought them to Trembling, who put them on. When Trembling was dressed and ready, the henwife said, "I have a honey-bird here to sit on your right shoulder, and a honey-finger to put on your left. At the door stands a milk-white mare, with a golden saddle for you to sit on, and a golden bridle to hold in your hand."

Trembling sat on the golden saddle, and when she was ready to start, the henwife said, "You must not go inside the door of the church, and the minute the people rise up at the end of Mass, do you make off, and ride home as fast as the mare will carry you."

When Trembling came to the door of the church there was no one inside who could get a glimpse of her but was striving to know who she was. When they saw her hurrying away at the end of Mass, they ran out to overtake her. But no use in their running; she was away before any man could come near her. From the minute she left the church till she got home, she overtook the wind before her, and outstripped the wind behind.

She came down at the door, went in, and found the henwife had dinner ready. She put off the white robes, and had on her old dress in a twinkling.

When the two sisters came home the henwife asked, "Have you any news today from the church?"

"We have great news," said they. "We saw a wonderful, grand lady at the church door. The like of the robes she had we have never seen on a woman before. It's little that was thought of our dresses beside what she had on. And there wasn't a man at the church, from the king to the beggar, but was trying to look at her and know who she was."

The sisters would give no peace till they had two dresses like the robes of the strange lady, but honey-birds and honey-fingers were not to be found.

Next Sunday the two sisters went to church again, and left the youngest at home to cook the dinner.

After they had gone, the henwife came in. "Will you go to church today?"

"I would go," said Trembling, "if I had another dress."

"What robe will you wear?" asked the henwife.

"The finest black satin that can be found, and red shoes for my feet."

"What color do you want the mare to be?"

"I want her to be so black and so glossy that I can see myself in her body."

The henwife put on the cloak of darkness, and asked for the robes and the mare. That moment she had them. When Trembling was dressed, the henwife put the honey-bird on her right shoulder and the honey-finger on her left. The saddle on the mare was silver, and so was the bridle.

When Trembling sat in the saddle and was going away, the henwife ordered her strictly not to go inside the door of the church, but to rush away as soon as the people rose at the end of Mass, and hurry home on the mare before any man could stop her.

That Sunday the people were more astonished than ever, and gazed at her more than the first time. All they were thinking of was to know who she was. But they had no chance, for the moment the people rose at the end of Mass she slipped from the church, was in the silver saddle, and home before a man could stop her or talk to her.

The henwife had the dinner ready. Trembling took off her satin robe, and had on her old clothes before her sisters got home.

"What news have you today?" asked the henwife of the sisters when they came from the church.

"Oh, we saw the grand strange lady again! And it's little that any man could think of our dresses after looking at the robes of satin that she had on! And all at church, from high to low, had their mouths open, gazing at her, and no man was looking at us."

The two sisters gave neither rest nor peace till they got dresses as nearly like the strange lady's robes as they could find. Of course they were not so good, for the like of those robes could not be found in Erin.

When the third Sunday came, Fair and Brown went to church dressed in black satin. They left Trembling at home to work in the kitchen, and told her to be sure and have dinner ready when they came back.

After they had gone and were out of sight, the henwife came to the kitchen. "Well, my dear, are you for church today?"

"I would go if I had a new dress to wear."

"I'll get you any dress you ask for. What dress would you like?"

"A dress red as a rose from the waist down, and white as snow from the waist up. A cape of green on my shoulders, and a hat on my head with a red, a white, and a green feather in it. And shoes for my feet with the toes red, the middle white, and the backs and heels green."

The henwife put on the cloak of darkness, wished for all these things, and had them. When Trembling was dressed, the henwife put the honey-bird on her right shoulder and the honey-finger on her left. Placing the hat on her head, she clipped a few hairs from one lock and a few from another with her scissors, and that moment the most beautiful golden hair was flowing down over the girl's shoulders. Then the henwife asked what kind of a mare she would ride. She said white, with blue and gold-colored diamond-shaped spots all over her body, on her back a saddle of gold, and on her head a golden bridle.

The mare stood there before the door, and a bird sitting between her ears, which began to sing as soon as Trembling was in the saddle, and never stopped till she came home from the church.

The fame of the beautiful strange lady had gone out through the world, and all the princes and great men that were in it came to church that Sunday, each one hoping that it was himself would have her home with him after Mass.

The son of the king of Omanya forgot all about the eldest sister, and remained outside the church, so as to catch the strange lady before she could hurry away.

The church was more crowded than ever before, and there were three times as many outside. There was such a throng before the church that Trembling could only come inside the gate.

As soon as the people were rising at the end of Mass, the lady slipped out through the gate, was in the golden saddle in an instant, and sweeping away ahead of the wind.

But if she was, the prince of Omanya was at her side, and, seizing her by the foot, he ran with the mare for thirty perches, and never let go of the beautiful lady till the shoe was pulled from her foot, and he was left behind with it in his hand. She came home as fast as the mare could carry her, and was thinking all the time that the henwife would kill her for losing the shoe.

Seeing her so vexed and so changed in the face, the old woman asked, "What's the trouble that's on you now?"

"Oh! I've lost one of the shoes off my feet," said Trembling.

"Don't mind that; don't be vexed. Maybe it's the best

thing that ever happened to you."

Trembling gave up all the things she had to the henwife, put on her old clothes, and went to work in the kitchen.

When the sisters came home, the henwife asked, "Have you any news from the church?"

"We have indeed," said they. "We saw the grandest sight today. The strange lady came again, in grander array than before. On herself and the horse she rode were the finest colors of the world, and between the ears of the horse was a bird which never stopped singing from the time she came till she went away. The lady herself is the most beautiful woman ever seen by man in Erin."

After Trembling had disappeared from the church, the son of the king of Omanya said to the other kings' sons, "I will have that lady for my own."

They all replied, "You didn't win her just by taking the shoe off her foot. You'll have to win her by the point of the sword. You'll have to fight for her with us before you can call her your own."

"Well," said the son of the king of Omanya, "when I find the lady that shoe will fit, I'll fight for her, never fear, before I leave her to any of you."

Then all the kings' sons were uneasy, and anxious to know who she was that lost the shoe, and they began to travel all over Erin to know could they find her. The prince of Omanya and all the others went in a great company together, and made the round of Erin. They went everywhere; north, south, east, and west. They visited every place where a woman was to be found, and left not a house in the kingdom they did not search, to know could they find the woman the shoe would fit, not caring whether she was rich or poor, of high or low degree.

The prince of Omanya always kept the shoe. When the young women saw it, they had great hopes, for it was of proper size, neither large nor small, and it would beat any man to know of what material it was made. One thought it would fit her if she cut a little from her great toe. Another, with too short a foot, put something in the tip of her stocking. But no use, they only spoiled their feet, and were curing them for months afterwards.

The two sisters, Fair and Brown, heard that the princes of the world were looking all over Erin for the woman that could wear the shoe, and every day they were talking of trying it on.

One day Trembling spoke up and said, "Maybe it's my foot that the shoe will fit."

"Oh, the breaking of the dog's foot on you! Why say so when you were at home every Sunday?"

They were that way waiting, and scolding the younger sister, till the princes were near the place. The day they were to come, the sisters put Trembling in a closet, and locked the door on her. When the company came to the house, the prince of Omanya gave the shoe to the sisters. But though they tried and tried, it would fit neither of them.

"Is there any other young woman in the house?" asked the prince.

"There is," said Trembling, speaking up in the closet. "I'm here."

"Oh! We have her for nothing but to put out the ashes," said the sisters.

But the prince and the others wouldn't leave the house till they had seen her, so the two sisters had to open the door. When Trembling came out, the shoe was given to her, and it fitted exactly.

The prince of Omanya looked at her and said, "You are the woman the shoe fits, and you are the woman I took the shoe from."

Trembling replied, "Do you stay here till I return."

Then she went to the henwife's house. The old woman put on the cloak of darkness, got everything for her she had the first Sunday at church, and put her on the white mare in the same fashion. Then Trembling rode along the highway to the front of the house. All who saw her the first time said, "This is the lady we saw at church."

Then she went away a second time, and a second time came back on the black mare in the second dress which the henwife gave her. All who saw her the second Sunday said, "That is the lady we saw at church."

A third time she asked for a short absence, and soon came back on the third mare and in the third dress. All who saw her the third time said, "That is the lady we saw at church."

Every man was satisfied, and knew that she was the woman.

Then all the princes and great men spoke up, and said to the son of the king of Omanya, "You'll have to fight now for her before we let her go with you."

"I'm here before you, ready for combat," answered the prince.

Then the son of the king of Lochlin stepped forth. The struggle began, and a terrible struggle it was. They fought for nine hours, and then the son of the king of Lochlin stopped, gave up his claim, and left the field. Next day the son of the king of Spain fought six hours, and yielded his claim. On the third day the son of the king of Nyerfói fought eight hours, and stopped. The fourth day the son of the king of Greece fought six hours, and stopped. On the fifth day no more strange princes wanted to fight, and all the sons of kings in Erin said they would not fight with a man of their own land, that the strangers had had their chance. And as no others came to claim the woman, she belonged of right to the son of the king of Omanya.

The marriage day was fixed, and the invitations sent out. The wedding lasted for a year and a day. When the wedding was over, the king's son brought home the bride, and when the time came a son was born. The young woman sent for her eldest sister, Fair, to be with her and care for her.

One day, when Trembling was well, and when her husband was away hunting, the two sisters went out to walk. When they came to the seaside, the eldest pushed the youngest sister in. A great whale came and swallowed her.

The eldest sister came home alone, and the husband asked, "Where is your sister?"

"She has gone home to her father in Ballyshannon. Now that I am well, I don't need her."

"Well," said the husband, looking closely at her, "I'm in dread it's my wife that has gone."

"Oh, no!" said she. "It's my sister Fair that's gone."

Since the sisters were very much alike, the prince was in doubt. That night he put his sword between them, and said, "If you are my wife, this sword will get warm. If not, it will stay cold."

In the morning when he rose up, the sword was as cold as when he put it there.

It happened when the two sisters were walking by the seashore, that a little cowherd was down by the water minding cattle, and saw Fair push Trembling into the sea. Next day, when the tide came in, he saw the whale swim up and throw her out on the sand.

She said to the cowherd, "When you go home in the evening with the cows, tell the master that my sister Fair pushed me into the sea yesterday. That a whale swallowed me, and then threw me out, but will come again and swallow me with the coming of the next tide. Then he'll go out with the tide, and come again with tomorrow's tide, and throw me again on the strand. The whale will cast me out three times.

I'm under the enchantment of this whale, and cannot leave the beach or escape myself. Unless my husband saves me before I'm swallowed the fourth time I shall be lost. He must come and shoot the whale with a silver bullet when he turns on the broad of his back. Under the breast-fin of the whale is a reddish-brown spot. My husband must hit him in that spot, for it is the only place in which he can be killed."

When the cowherd got home, the eldest sister gave him a draught of oblivion, and he did not tell. Next day he went again to the sea. The whale came and cast Trembling on shore again.

She asked the boy, "Did you tell the master what I told you to tell him?"

"I did not," said he. "I forgot."

"How did you forget?" asked she.

"The woman of the house gave me a drink that made me forget."

"Well, don't forget telling him this night, and if she gives you a drink, don't take it from her."

As soon as the cowherd came home, the eldest sister offered him a drink. He refused to take it till be had delivered his message and told all to the master.

The third day the prince went down with his gun and a silver bullet in it. He was not long down when the whale came and threw Trembling upon the beach as the two days before. She had no power to speak to her husband till he had killed the whale. Then the whale went out, turned over once on the broad of his back, and showed the spot for a moment only. That moment the prince fired. He had but the one chance, and a short one at that. But he took it, and hit the spot, and the whale, mad with pain, made the sea all around red with blood, and died.

That minute Trembling was able to speak, and went home with her husband, who sent word to her father what the eldest sister had done. The father came, and told him any death he chose to give her to give it. The prince told the father he would leave her life and death with himself. The father had her put out then on the sea in a barrel, with provisions in it for seven years.

In time Trembling had a second child; a daughter. The prince and she sent the cowherd to school, and trained him up as one of their own children, and said, "If the little girl that is born to us now lives, no other man in the world will get her but him."

The cowherd and the prince's daughter lived on till they were married. The mother said to her husband, "You could not have saved me from the whale but for the little cowherd. On that account I don't grudge him my daughter."

The son of the king of Omanya and Trembling had fourteen children, and they lived happily till the two died of old age.

17.

THE TALE OF VIVIONN
THE GIANTESS

ONE DAY Finn and Goll, Keelta and Oscar, and others of
the Fianna, were resting after the hunt on a certain hill now
called the Ridge of the Dead Woman. Their meal was being
got ready, when a girl of the kin of the giants came striding
up and sat down among them.

"Didst thou ever see a woman so tall?" asked Finn of
Goll.

"By my troth," replied Goll, "never have I or any other
seen a woman so big."

She took her hand out of her bosom and on her long
slender fingers there were three gold rings, each as thick as
an ox's yoke.

"Let us question her," said Goll.

Finn said, "If we stood up, perchance she might hear
us."

So they all rose to their feet, but the giantess, on that,
rose up too.

"Maiden," said Finn. "If thou have aught to say to us or
to hear from us, sit down and lean thine elbow on the
hillside."

So she lay down and Finn bade her say whence she came

and what was her will with them.

"Out of the World Oversea where the sun sets am I come," she said. "To seek thy protection, oh mighty Finn."

"And what is thy name?"

"My name is Vivionn of the Fair Hair, and my father Treon is called King of the Land of Lasses. He has but three sons and nine and seven score daughters. Near him is a King who hath one daughter and eight score sons. To one of these, Æda, was I given in marriage sorely against my will. Three times now have I fled from him. And this time it was fishermen whom the wind blew to us from off this land who told us of a mighty lord here, named Finn, son of Cuill, who would let none be wronged or oppressed, but he would be their friend and champion. And if thou be he, to thee am I come."

She laid her hand in Finn's' and he bade her do the same with Goll mac Morna, who was second in the Fian leadership, and she did so.

Then the maiden took from her head a jeweled golden helmet, and immediately her hair flowed out in seven score tresses, fair, curly and golden, at the abundance of which all stood amazed.

Finn said, "By the Immortals that we adore, but King Cormac and the poetess Ethne and the fair women-folk of the Fianna would deem it a marvel to see this girl. Tell us now, maiden, what portion wilt thou have of meat and drink? Will that of a hundred of us suffice thee?"

The girl then saw Cnu, the dwarf harper of Finn, who had just been playing to them. "Whatever thou givest to yon little man that bears the harp, be it much or little, the same, oh Finn, will suffice for me."

Then she begged a drink from them, and Finn called his gillie, Saltran, and bade him fetch the full of a certain great goblet with water from the ford. Now, this goblet was of wood, and it held as much as nine of the Fianna could drink. The maiden poured some of the water into her right hand and drank three sips of it, and scattered the rest over the Fianna, and she and they burst out laughing.

Finn said, "On thy conscience, girl, what ailed thee not to drink out of the goblet?"

"Never," she replied, "have I drunk out of any vessel but there was a rim of gold to it, or at least of silver."

And now Keelta looking up, perceived a tall youth coming swiftly towards them, who, when he approached, seemed even bigger than was the maiden. He wore a rough hairy cape over his shoulder and beneath that a green cloak fastened by a golden brooch. His tunic was of royal satin, and he bore a red shield slung over his shoulders, and a spear with a shaft as thick as a man's leg was in his hand, and a gold-hilted sword hung by his side. And his face, which was smooth-shaven, was comelier than that of any of the sons of men.

When he came near, seeing among the Fians a stir of alarm at this apparition, Finn said, "Keep every one of you his place, and let neither warrior nor gillie address him. Know any of you this champion?"

"I know him," said the maiden. "That is even he to escape from whom I am come to thee, oh Finn."

She sat down between Finn and Goll. But the stranger drew near, and spake never a word. Before anyone could tell what he would be at, he thrust fiercely and suddenly with his spear at the girl, and the shaft stood out a hand's breadth at her back. She fell gasping, but the young man drew his weapon out and passed rapidly through the crowd and away.

Red with wrath, Finn cried, "Ye have seen! Avenge this wicked deed, or none of you aspire to Fianship again."

The whole company sprang to their feet and gave chase to that murderer, save only Finn and Goll, who stayed by the dying maiden. They ran him by hill and plain to the great Bay of Tralee and down to the Tribute Point, where the traders from oversea were wont to pay their dues, and there he set his face to the West and took the water.

By this time four of the Fianna had outstripped the rest, namely, Keelta, and Dermot, and Glas, and Oscar, son of Oisín. Of these Keelta was first, and just as the giant was mid-leg in the waves he hurled his spear and it severed the thong of the giant's shield so that it fell off in the water. As the giant paused, Keelta seized his spear and tore it from him. But the giant waded on, and soon the Fians were floundering in deep water while the huge form, thigh deep, was seen striding towards the setting sun. A great ship seemed to draw near, and it received him, and then departed into the light.

The Fians returned in the grey evening, bearing the spear and the great shield to Finn. There they found the maiden at point of death, and they laid the weapons before her.

"Goodly indeed are these arms," she said. "For that is the Thunder Spear of the King Oversea and the shield is the Red Branch Shield." It was covered with red arabesques. Then she bestowed her bracelets on Finn's three harpers, the dwarf Cnu, and Blanit his wife, and the harper Daira. And she bade Finn care for her burial, that it should be done becomingly. "For under thy honor and protection I got my death, and it was to thee I came into Ireland."

So they buried her and lamented her, and made a great far-seen mound over her grave, which is called the Ridge of the Dead Woman, and set up a pillar stone upon it with her name and lineage carved in Ogham-crave.

18.

CONNLA AND THE FAERY MAIDEN

CONNLA OF THE Fiery Hair was son of Conn of the Hundred Fights. One day as he stood by the side of his father on the height of Usna, he saw a maiden clad in strange attire coming towards him.

"Whence comest thou, maiden?" he asked.

"I come from the Plains of the Ever Living," she said. "There where there is neither death nor sin. There we keep holiday always, nor need we help from any in our joy. And in all our pleasure we have no strife. And because we have our homes in the round green hills, men call us the Hill Folk."

The king and all with him wondered much to hear a voice when they saw no one. For save Connla alone, none saw the Faery Maiden.

"To whom art thou talking, my son?" asked Conn the king.

Then the maiden answered, "Connla speaks to a young, fair maid, whom neither death nor old age awaits. I love Connla, and now I call him away to the Plain of Pleasure, Moy Mell, where Boadag is king for aye, nor has there been complaint or sorrow in that land since he has held the kingship. Oh, come with me, Connla of the Fiery Hair, ruddy as the dawn with thy tawny skin. A faery crown awaits thee to grace thy comely face and royal form. Come, and never shall thy comeliness fade, nor thy youth, till the last awful day of judgment."

The king in fear at what the maiden said, which he heard though he could not see her, called aloud to his Druid, Coran by name.

"Oh, Coran of the many spells and of the cunning magic, I call upon thy aid. A task is upon me too great for all my skill and wit, greater than any laid upon me since I seized the kingship. A maiden unseen has met us, and by her power would take from me my dear, my comely son. If thou help not, he will be taken from thy king by woman's wiles and witchery."

Coran the Druid stood forth and chanted his spells towards the spot where the maiden's voice had been heard. And none heard her voice again, nor could Connla see her longer. Only as she vanished before the Druid's mighty spell, she threw an apple to Connla. For a whole month from that day Connla would take nothing, either to eat or to drink, save only from that apple. But as he ate, it grew again and always kept whole. And all the while there grew within him a mighty yearning and longing after the maiden he had seen.

When the last day of the month of waiting came, Connla stood by the side of the king his father on the Plain of Arcomin, and again he saw the maiden come towards him, and again she spoke to him.

"'Tis a glorious place, forsooth, that Connla holds among short-lived mortals awaiting the day of death. But now the folk of life, the ever-living ones, beg and bid thee come to Moy Mell, the Plain of Pleasure, for they have learnt to know thee, seeing thee in thy home among thy dear ones."

When Conn the king heard the maiden's voice he called

to his men. "Summon swift my Druid Coran, for I see she has again this day the power of speech."

The maiden said, "Oh, mighty Conn, fighter of a hundred fights, the Druid's power is little loved. It has little honor in the mighty land, peopled with so many of the upright. When the Law will come, it will do away with the Druid's magic spells that come from the lips of the false black demon."

Conn the king observed that since the maiden came, Connla, his son spoke to none that spake to him. So Conn of the hundred fights said to him, "Is it to thy mind what the woman says, my son?"

"Tis hard upon me," then said Connla. "I love my own folk above all things, but yet... but yet a longing seizes me for the maiden."

When the maiden heard this, she answered, "The ocean is not so strong as the waves of thy longing. Come with me in my *curragh,* the gleaming, straight-gliding crystal canoe. Soon we can reach Boadag's realm. I see the bright sun sink, yet far as it is, we can reach it before dark. There is, too, another land worthy of thy journey, a land joyous to all that seek it. Only wives and maidens dwell there. If thou wilt, we can seek it and live there alone together in joy." When the maiden ceased to speak, Connla of the Fiery Hair rushed away from them and sprang into the *curragh*, the gleaming, straight-gliding crystal canoe. And then they all, king and court, saw it glide away over the bright sea towards the setting sun. Away and away, till eye could see it no longer, and Connla and the Faery Maiden went their way on the sea, and were no more seen, nor did any know where they came.

19.

HUDDEN AND DUDDEN
AND DONALD O'NEARY

THERE WAS once upon a time two farmers, and their names were Hudden and Dudden. They had poultry in their yards, sheep on the uplands, and scores of cattle in the meadow land alongside the river. But for all that they weren't happy. For just between their two farms there lived a poor man by the name of Donald O'Neary. He had a hovel over his head and a strip of grass that was barely enough to keep his one cow, Daisy, from starving. And though she did her best, it was but seldom that Donald got a drink of milk or a roll of butter from Daisy. You would think there was little here to make Hudden and Dudden jealous, but so it is, the more one has the more one wants, and Donald's neighbors lay awake of nights scheming how they might get hold of his little strip of grass land. Daisy, poor thing, they never thought of; she was just a bag of bones.

One day Hudden met Dudden, and they were soon grumbling as usual, and all to the tune of, "If only we could get that vagabond Donald O'Neary out of the country."

"Let's kill Daisy," said Hudden at last. "If that doesn't make him clear out, nothing will."

No sooner said than agreed, and it wasn't dark before

Hudden and Dudden crept up to the little shed where lay poor Daisy trying her best to chew the cud, though she hadn't had as much grass in the day as would cover your hand. And when Donald came to see if Daisy was all snug for the night, the poor beast had only time to lick his hand once before she died.

Well, Donald was a shrewd fellow, and downhearted though he was, began to think if he could get any good out of Daisy's death. He thought and he thought, and the next day you could have seen him trudging off early to the fair, Daisy's hide over his shoulder, every penny he had jingling in his pockets. Just before he got to the fair, he made several slits in the hide, put a penny in each slit, walked into the best inn of the town as bold as if it belonged to him, and hanging the hide up to a nail in the wall, sat down.

"Some of your best whiskey," says he to the landlord. But the landlord didn't like his looks. "Is it fearing I won't pay you, you are?" says Donald. "Why, I have a hide here that gives me all the money I want." And with that he hit it a whack with his stick and out hopped a penny.

The landlord opened his eyes, as you may fancy. "What'll you take for that hide?"

"It's not for sale, my good man."

"Will you take a gold piece?"

"It's not for sale, I tell you. Hasn't it kept me and mine for years?" With that Donald hit the hide another whack and out jumped a second penny.

Well, the long and the short of it was that Donald let the hide go, and that very evening, who but he should walk up to Hudden's door?

"Good evening, Hudden. Will you lend me your best pair of scales?"

Hudden stared and scratched his head, but he lent the scales.

When Donald was safe at home, he pulled out his pocketful of bright gold and began to weigh each piece in the scales. But Hudden had put a lump of butter at the bottom, and so the last piece of gold stuck fast to the scales when he took them back to Hudden.

If Hudden had stared before, he stared ten times more now, and no sooner was Donald's back turned, than he was of as hard as he could pelt to Dudden's.

"Good evening, Dudden. That vagabond, bad luck to him."

"You mean Donald O'Neary?"

"And who else should I mean? He's back here weighing out sacksful of gold."

"How do you know that?"

"Here are my scales that he borrowed, and here's a gold piece still sticking to them."

Off they went together, and they came to Donald's door. Donald had finished making the last pile of ten gold pieces. And he couldn't finish because a piece had stuck to the scales.

In they walked without an "If you please," or "By your leave."

"Well, I never!" That was all they could say.

"Good evening, Hudden. Good evening, Dudden. Ah! You thought you had played me a fine trick, but you never did me a better turn in all your lives. When I found poor Daisy dead, I thought to myself, 'Well, her hide may fetch something,' and it did. Hides are worth their weight in gold in the market just now."

Hudden nudged Dudden, and Dudden winked at Hudden.

"Good evening, Donald O'Neary."

"Good evening, kind friends."

The next day there wasn't a cow or a calf that belonged

to Hudden or Dudden, but her hide was going to the fair in Hudden's biggest cart drawn by Dudden's strongest pair of horses.

When they came to the fair, each one took a hide over his arm, and there they were walking through the fair, bawling out at the top of their voices: "Hides to sell! Hides to sell!"

Out came the tanner. "How much for your hides, my good men?"

"Their weight in gold."

"It's early in the day to come out of the tavern." That was all the tanner said, and back he went to his yard.

"Hides to sell! Fine fresh hides to sell!"

Out came the cobbler. "How much for your hides, my men?"

"Their weight in gold."

"Is it making game of me you are! Take that for your pains." The cobbler dealt Hudden a blow that made him stagger.

Up the people came running from one end of the fair to the other. "What's the matter? What's the matter?" cried they.

"Here are a couple of vagabonds selling hides at their weight in gold," said the cobbler.

"Hold 'e' fast! Hold 'e' fast!" bawled the innkeeper, who was the last to come up, he was so fat. "I'll wager it's one of the rogues who tricked me out of thirty gold pieces yesterday for a wretched hide."

It was more kicks than halfpence that Hudden and Dudden got before they were well on their way home again, and they didn't run the slower because all the dogs of the town were at their heels.

Well, as you may fancy, if they loved Donald little before, they loved him less now.

"What's the matter, friends?" said he, as he saw them tearing along, their hats knocked in, and their coats torn off, and their faces black and blue. "Is it fighting you've been? Or mayhap you met the police, ill luck to them?"

"We'll police you, you vagabond. It's mighty smart you thought yourself, deluding us with your lying tales."

"Who deluded you? Didn't you see the gold with your own two eyes?"

But it was no use talking. Pay for it he must, and should. There was a meal sack handy, and into it Hudden and Dudden popped Donald O'Neary, tied him up tight and ran a pole through the knot. Off they started for the Brown Lake of the Bog, each with a pole end on his shoulder, and Donald O'Neary between.

But the Brown Lake was far, the road was dusty, Hudden and Dudden were sore and weary, and parched with thirst. There was an inn by the roadside.

"Let's go in," said Hudden. "I'm dead beat. It's heavy he is for the little he had to eat."

If Hudden was willing, so was Dudden. As for Donald, you may be sure his leave wasn't asked, but he was lumped down at the inn door for all the world as if he had been a sack of potatoes.

"Sit still, you vagabond," said Dudden. "If we don't mind waiting, you needn't'"

Donald held his peace, but after a while he heard the glasses clink, and Hudden singing away at the top of his voice.

"I won't have her, I tell you. I won't have her!" said Donald. But nobody heeded what he said.

"I won't have her, I tell you. I won't have her!" repeated Donald, and this time he said it louder, but nobody heeded what he said.

"I won't have her, I tell you. I won't have her!" said

Donald again. This time he said it as loud as he could.

"And who won't you have, may I be so bold as to ask?" said a farmer, who had just come up with a drove of cattle, and was turning in for a glass.

"It's the king's daughter. They are bothering the life out of me to marry her."

"You're the lucky fellow. I'd give something to be in your shoes."

"Do you see that, now! Wouldn't it be a fine thing for a farmer to be marrying a princess, all dressed in gold and jewels?"

"Jewels, do you say? Ah, now, couldn't you take me with you?"

"Well, you're an honest fellow. As I don't care for the king's daughter, though she's as beautiful as the day, and is covered with jewels from top to toe, you shall have her. Just undo the cord, and let me out. They tied me up tight, as they knew I'd run away from her."

Out crawled Donald; in crept the farmer.

"Now, lie still, and don't mind the shaking. It's only rumbling over the palace steps you'll be. And maybe they'll abuse you for a vagabond, who won't have the king's daughter, but you needn't mind that. Ah! It's a deal I'm giving up for you, sure as it is that I don't care for the princess."

"Take my cattle in exchange," said the farmer, and you may guess it wasn't long before Donald was at their tails driving them homewards.

Out came Hudden and Dudden, and the one took one end of the pole, and the other the other.

"I'm thinking he's heavier," said Hudden.

"Ah, never mind," said Dudden. "It's only a step now to the Brown Lake."

"I'll have her now! I'll have her now!" bawled the farmer from inside the sack.

"By my faith, and you shall, though," said Hudden, and he laid his stick across the sack.

"I'll have her! I'll have her!" bawled the farmer, louder than ever.

"Well, here you are," said Dudden, for they were now come to the Brown Lake, and, unslinging the sack, they pitched it plump into the lake.

"You'll not be playing your tricks on us any longer," said Hudden.

"True for you," said Dudden. "Ah, Donald, my boy, it was an ill day when you borrowed my scales."

Off they went, with a light step and an easy heart. But when they were near home, who should they see but Donald O'Neary, and all around him the cows were grazing, and the calves were kicking up their heels and butting their heads together.

"Is it you, Donald?" asked Dudden. "Faith, you've been quicker than we have."

"True for you, Dudden, and let me thank you kindly. The turn was good, if the will was ill. You'll have heard like me, that the Brown Lake leads to the Land of Promise. I always put it down as lies, but it is just as true as my word. Look at the cattle."

Hudden stared, and Dudden gaped. They couldn't get over the cattle; fine fat cattle they were, too.

"It's only the worst I could bring up with me," said Donald O'Neary. "The others were so fat, there was no driving them. Faith, too, it's little wonder they didn't care to leave, with grass as far as you could see, and as sweet and juicy as fresh butter."

"Ah, now, Donald, we haven't always been friends," said Dudden. "But as I was just saying, you were ever a decent lad, and you'll show us the way?"

"I don't see that I'm called upon to do that. There is a

power more cattle down there. Why shouldn't I have them all to myself?"

"Faith, they may well say, the richer you get, the harder the heart. You always were a neighborly lad, Donald. You wouldn't wish to keep the luck all to yourself?"

"True for you, Hudden, though it's a bad example you set me. But I'll not be thinking of old times. There is plenty for all there, so come along with me."

Off they trudged, with a light heart and an eager step. When they came to the Brown Lake, the sky was full of little white clouds, and, if the sky was full, the lake was as full.

"Ah! Now, look, there they are," cried Donald, as he pointed to the clouds in the lake.

"Where? Where?" cried Hudden.

"Don't be greedy!" cried Dudden, as he jumped his hardest to be up first with the fat cattle. But if he jumped first, Hudden wasn't long behind.

They never came back. Maybe they got too fat, like the cattle. As for Donald O'Neary, he had cattle and sheep all his days to his heart's content.

20.

GULEESH

THERE WAS once a boy in the County Mayo; Guleesh was his name. There was the finest *rath* a little way off from the gable of the house, and he was often in the habit of seating himself on the fine grass bank that was running round it. One night he stood, half leaning against the gable of the house, and looking up into the sky, and watching the beautiful white moon over his head.

After he had been standing that way for a couple of hours, he said to himself, "My bitter grief that I am not gone away out of this place altogether. I'd sooner be any place in the world than here. Och, it's well for you, white moon," says he, "that's turning round, turning round, as you please yourself, and no man can put you back. I wish I was the same as you."

Hardly was the word out of his mouth when he heard a great noise coming like the sound of many people running together, and talking, and laughing, and making sport. The sound went by him like a whirl of wind, and he was listening to it going into the *rath*.

"*Musha*, by my soul," says he. "But ye're merry enough, and I'll follow ye."

What was in it but the faery host, though he did not know at first that it was they, and he followed them into the *rath*. It's there he heard the fulparnee, and the folpornee, the rap-lay-hoota, and the roolya-boolya, that they had there, and every man of them crying out as loud as he could: "My horse, and bridle, and saddle! My horse, and bridle, and saddle!"

"By my hand," said Guleesh. "My boy, that's not bad. I'll imitate ye." He cried out as well as they, "My horse, and bridle, and saddle! My horse, and bridle, and saddle!"

And on the moment there was a fine horse with a bridle of gold, and a saddle of silver, standing before him. He leaped up on it, and the moment he was on its back he saw clearly that the *rath* was full of horses, and of little people going riding on them.

Said a man of them to him, "Are you coming with us tonight, Guleesh?"

"I am, surely," said Guleesh.

"If you are, come along," said the little man.

Out they went all together, riding like the wind, faster than the fastest horse ever you saw a-hunting, and faster than the fox and the hounds at his tail.

The cold winter wind that was before them, they overtook her, and the cold winter wind that was behind them, she did not overtake them. And stop nor stay of that full race, did they make none, until they came to the brink of the sea.

Then every one of them said, "Hie over cap! Hie over cap!" And that moment they were up in the air, and before Guleesh had time to remember where he was, they were down on dry land again, and were going like the wind.

At last they stood still, and a man of them said to Guleesh, "Guleesh, do you know where you are now?"

"Not a know," says Guleesh.

"You're in France, Guleesh," said he. "The daughter of the king of France is to be married tonight, the handsomest woman that the sun ever saw. We must do our best to bring her with us, if we're only able to carry her off. You must come with us that we may be able to put the young girl up behind you on the horse, when we'll be bringing her away, for it's not lawful for us to put her sitting behind ourselves. But you're flesh and blood, and she can take a good grip of you, so that she won't fall off the horse. Are you satisfied, Guleesh, and will you do what we're telling you?"

"Why shouldn't I be satisfied?" answered Guleesh. "I'm satisfied, surely, and anything that ye will tell me to do I'll do it without doubt."

They got off their horses there, and a man of them said a word that Guleesh did not understand. On the moment they were lifted up, and Guleesh found himself and his companions in the palace. There was a great feast going on there, and there was not a nobleman or a gentleman in the kingdom but was gathered there, dressed in silk and satin, and gold and silver. The night was as bright as the day with all the lamps and candles that were lit, and Guleesh had to shut his two eyes at the brightness. When he opened them again and looked, he thought he never saw anything as fine as all he saw there. There were a hundred tables spread out, and full of meat and drink on each table of them, flesh-meat, and cakes and sweetmeats, and wine and ale, and every drink that ever a man saw. The musicians were at the two ends of the hall, and they were playing the sweetest music that ever a man's ear heard. There were young women and fine youths in the middle of the hall, dancing and turning, and going round so quickly and so lightly, that it put a *soorawn* in Guleesh's head to be looking at them. There were more there playing tricks, and more making fun and laughing, for such a feast as there was that day had not been in France for twenty years, because the old king had no children alive but only the one daughter, and she was to be married to the son of another king that night. Three days the feast was going on, and the third night she was to be married, and that was the night that Guleesh and the *sheehogues* came, hoping if they could, to carry off with them the king's young daughter.

Guleesh and his companions were standing together at the head of the hall, where there was a fine altar dressed up, and two bishops behind it waiting to marry the girl as soon as the right time should come. Now nobody could see the *sheehogues,* for they said a word as they came in that made them all invisible, as if they had not been in it at all.

"Tell me which of them is the king's daughter," said Guleesh, when he was becoming a little used to the noise and the light.

"Don't you see her there away from you?" said the little man that he was talking to.

Guleesh looked where the little man was pointing with his finger, and there he saw the loveliest woman that was, he thought, upon the ridge of the world. The rose and the lily were fighting together in her face, and one could not tell which of them got the victory. Her arms and hands were like the lime, her mouth as red as a strawberry when it is ripe, her foot was as small and as light as another one's hand, her form was smooth and slender, and her hair was falling down from her head in buckles of gold. Her garments and dress were woven with gold and silver, and the bright stone that was in the ring on her hand was as shining as the sun.

Guleesh was nearly blinded with all the loveliness and beauty that was in her, but when he looked again, he saw that she was crying, and that there was the trace of tears in her eyes.

"It can't be," said Guleesh, "that there's grief on her, when everybody round her is so full of sport and merriment."

"*Musha,* then, she is grieved," said the little man. "For

it's against her own will she's marrying, and she has no love for the husband she is to marry. The king was going to give her to him three years ago, when she was only fifteen, but she said she was too young, and requested him to leave her as she was yet. The king gave her a year's grace, and when that year was up he gave her another year's grace, and then another. But a week or a day he would not give her longer, and she is eighteen years old tonight, and it's time for her to marry. But indeed," says he, and he crooked his mouth in an ugly way. "Indeed, it's no king's son she'll marry, if I can help it."

Guleesh pitied the handsome young lady greatly when he heard that, and he was heartbroken to think that it would be necessary for her to marry a man she did not like, or what was worse, to take a nasty sheehogue for a husband. However, he did not say a word, though he could not help giving many a curse to the ill luck that was laid out for himself, to be helping the people that were to snatch her away from her home and from her father.

He began thinking then, what it was he ought to do to save her, but he could think of nothing. "Oh! If I could only give her some help and relief," said he. "I wouldn't care whether I were alive or dead. But I see nothing that I can do for her."

He was looking on when the king's son came up to her and asked her for a kiss, but she turned her head away from him. Guleesh had double pity for her then, when he saw the lad taking her by the soft white hand, and drawing her out to dance. They went round in the dance near where Guleesh was, and he could plainly see that there were tears in her eyes.

When the dancing was over, the old king, her father, and her mother the queen, came up and said that this was the right time to marry her. The bishop was ready, and it was time to put the wedding ring on her and give her to her husband.

The king took the youth by the hand, and the queen took her daughter, and they went up together to the altar, with the lords and great people following them.

When they came near the altar, and were no more than about four yards from it, the little sheehogue stretched out his foot before the girl, and she fell. Before she was able to rise again he threw something that was in his hand upon her, said a couple of words, and upon the moment the maiden was gone from amongst them. Nobody could see her, for that word made her invisible. The little man seized her and raised her up behind Guleesh, and the king nor no one else saw them, but out with them through the hall till they came to the door.

Oro! Dear Mary! It's there the pity was, and the trouble, and the crying, and the wonder, and the searching, and the *rookawn*, when that lady disappeared from their eyes, and without their seeing what did it. Out of the door of the palace they went, without being stopped or hindered, for nobody saw them.

"My horse, my bridle, and saddle!" says every man of them.

"My horse, my bridle, and saddle!" says Guleesh, and on the moment the horse was standing ready caparisoned before him.

"Now, jump up, Guleesh," said the little man, "and put the lady behind you, and we will be going. The morning is not far off from us now."

Guleesh raised her up on the horse's back, and leaped up himself before her. "Rise, horse," said he, and his horse, and the other horses with him went in a full race until they came to the sea.

"Hie over cap!" said every man of them.

"Hie over cap!" said Guleesh, and on the moment the

horse rose under him, and cut a leap in the clouds, and came down in Erin.

They did not stop there, but went of a race to the place where was Guleesh's house and the *rath*. And when they came as far as that, Guleesh turned and caught the young girl in his two arms, and leaped off the horse.

"I call and cross you to myself, in the name of God!" said he. On the spot, before the word was out of his mouth, the horse fell down. And what was in it but the beam of a plough, of which they had made a horse, and every other horse they had, it was that way they made it. Some of them were riding on an old besom, and some on a broken stick, and more on a *bohalawn* or a hemlock-stalk.

The good people called out together when they heard what Guleesh said. "Oh! Guleesh, you clown, you thief, that no good may happen you, why did you play that trick on us?"

But they had no power at all to carry off the girl, after Guleesh had consecrated her to himself.

"Oh! Guleesh, isn't that a nice turn you did us, and we so kind to you? What good have we now out of our journey to France? Never mind yet, you clown, but you'll pay us another time for this. Believe us, you'll repent it."

"He'll have no good to get out of the young girl," said the little man that was talking to him in the palace before that. As he said the word he moved over to her and struck her a slap on the side of the head. "Now," says he, "she'll be without talk anymore. Guleesh, what good will she be to you when she'll be dumb? It's time for us to go, but you'll remember us, Guleesh!"

When he said that he stretched out his two hands, and before Guleesh was able to give an answer, he and the rest of them were gone into the *rath* out of his sight, and he saw them no more.

He turned to the young woman and said to her. "Thanks

be to God, they're gone. Would you not sooner stay with me than with them?" She gave him no answer. "There's trouble and grief on her yet," said Guleesh in his own mind. He spoke to her again. "I am afraid that you must spend this night in my father's house, lady, and if there is anything that I can do for you, tell me, and I'll be your servant."

The beautiful girl remained silent, but there were tears in her eyes, and her face was white and red after each other.

"Lady," said Guleesh, "tell me what you would like me to do now. I never belonged at all to that lot of *sheehogues* who carried you away with them. I am the son of an honest farmer, and I went with them without knowing it. If I'll be able to send you back to your father I'll do it, and I pray you make any use of me now that you may wish."

He looked into her face, and he saw the mouth moving as if she was going to speak, but there came no word from it.

"It cannot be," said Guleesh, "that you are dumb. Did I not hear you speaking to the king's son in the palace tonight? Or has that devil made you really dumb, when he struck his nasty hand on your jaw?"

The girl raised her white smooth hand, and laid her finger on her tongue, to show him that she had lost her voice and power of speech. The tears ran out of her two eyes like streams, and Guleesh's own eyes were not dry, for as rough as he was on the outside he had a soft heart, and could not stand the sight of the young girl, and she in that unhappy plight.

He began thinking with himself what he ought to do, and he did not like to bring her home with himself to his father's house, for he knew well that they would not believe him, that he had been in France and brought back with him the king of France's daughter. He was afraid they might make a mock of the young lady or insult her.

As he was doubting what he ought to do, and hesitating, he chanced to remember the priest. "Glory be to God," said he. "I know now what I'll do. I'll bring her to the priest's house, and he won't refuse me to keep the lady and care for her." He turned to the lady again and told her that he was loth to take her to his father's house, but that there was an excellent priest very friendly to himself, who would take good care of her, if she wished to remain in his house. But that if there was any other place she would rather go, he said he would bring her to it.

She bent her head to show him she was obliged, and gave him to understand that she was ready to follow him any place he was going.

"We will go to the priest's house, then," said he. "He is under an obligation to me, and will do anything I ask him."

They went together accordingly to the priest's house, and the sun was just rising when they came to the door. Guleesh beat it hard, and as early as it was the priest was up, and opened the door himself. He wondered when he saw Guleesh and the girl, for he was certain that it was coming wanting to be married they were.

"Guleesh, Guleesh, isn't it the nice boy you are that you can't wait till ten o'clock or till twelve, but that you must be coming to me at this hour, looking for marriage, you and your sweetheart? You ought to know that I can't marry you at such a time, or, at all events, can't marry you lawfully. But ubbubboo!" said he, suddenly, as he looked again at the young girl. "In the name of God, who have you here? Who is she, or how did you get her?"

"Father," said Guleesh, "you can marry me, or anybody else, if you wish. But it's not looking for marriage I came to you now, but to ask you, if you please, to give a lodging in your house to this young lady."

The priest looked at him as though he had ten heads on

him, but without putting any other question to him, he desired him to come in, himself and the maiden, and when they came in, he shut the door, brought them into the parlor, and put them sitting.

"Now, Guleesh. Tell me truly who is this young lady, and whether you're out of your senses really, or are only making a joke of me."

"I'm not telling a word of lie, nor making a joke of you," said Guleesh. "But it was from the palace of the king of France I carried off this lady, and she is the daughter of the king of France."

He began his story then, and told the whole to the priest, and the priest was so much surprised that he could not help calling out at times, or clapping his hands together.

When Guleesh said from what he saw he thought the girl was not satisfied with the marriage that was going to take place in the palace before he and the *sheehogues* broke it up, there came a red blush into the girl's cheek. He was more certain than ever that she had sooner be as she was, badly as she was, than be the married wife of the man she hated. When Guleesh said that he would be very thankful to the priest if he would keep her in his own house, the kind man said he would do that as long as Guleesh pleased, but that he did not know what they ought to do with her, because they had no means of sending her back to her father again.

Guleesh answered that he was uneasy about the same thing, and that he saw nothing to do but to keep quiet until they should find some opportunity of doing something better. They made it up then between themselves that the priest should let on that it was his brother's daughter he had, who was come on a visit to him from another county, and that he should tell everybody that she was dumb, and do his best to keep everyone away from her. They told the young girl what it was they intended to do, and she showed by her eyes that she was obliged to them.

Guleesh went home then, and when his people asked him where he had been, he said that he had been asleep at the foot of the ditch, and had passed the night there.

There was great wonderment on the priest's neighbors at the girl who came so suddenly to his house without anyone knowing where she was from, or what business she had there. Some of the people said that everything was not as it ought to be. Others said that Guleesh was not like the same man that was in it before, and that it was a great story, how he was drawing every day to the priest's house, and that the priest had a wish and a respect for him, a thing they could not clear up at all.

That was true for them, indeed. For it was seldom the day went by but Guleesh would go to the priest's house, and have a talk with him, and as often as he would come he used to hope to find the young lady well again, and with leave to speak. But, alas! She remained dumb and silent, without relief or cure. Since she had no other means of talking, she carried on a sort of conversation between herself and himself, by moving her hand and fingers, winking her eyes, opening and shutting her mouth, laughing or smiling, and a thousand other signs, so that it was not long until they understood each other very well. Guleesh was always thinking how he should send her back to her father. But there was no one to go with her, and he himself did not know what road to go, for he had never been out of his own country before the night he brought her away with him. Nor had the priest any better knowledge than he. But when Guleesh asked him, he wrote three or four letters to the king of France, and gave them to buyers and sellers of wares, who used to be going from place to place across the sea. But they all went astray and never a one came to the king's hand.

This was the way they were for many months, and

Guleesh was falling deeper and deeper in love with her every day, and it was plain to himself and the priest that she liked him. The boy feared greatly at last, lest the king should really hear where his daughter was, and take her back from himself, and he besought the priest to write no more, but to leave the matter to God.

So they passed the time for a year, until there came a day when Guleesh was lying by himself, on the grass, on the last day of the last month in autumn. He was thinking over again in his own mind of everything that happened to him from the day that he went with the *sheehogues* across the sea. He remembered then, suddenly, that it was one November night that he was standing at the gable of the house, when the whirlwind came, and the *sheehogues* in it, and he said to himself, "We have November night again today, and I'll stand in the same place I was last year, until I see if the good people come again. Perhaps I might see or hear something that would be useful to me, and might bring back her talk again to Mary." That was the name himself and the priest called the king's daughter, for neither of them knew her right name. He told his intention to the priest, and the priest gave him his blessing.

Guleesh accordingly went to the old *rath* when the night was darkening, and he stood with his bent elbow leaning on a grey old flag, waiting till the middle of the night should come. The moon rose slowly, and it was like a knob of fire behind him. There was a white fog which was raised up over the fields of grass and all damp places, through the coolness of the night after a great heat in the day. The night was calm as is a lake when there is not a breath of wind to move a wave on it. There was no sound to be heard but the *cronawn* of the insects that would go by from time to time, or the hoarse sudden scream of the wild geese as they passed from lake to lake, half a mile up in the air over his head. Or the sharp whistle of the golden and green plover, rising and lying, lying and rising, as they do on a calm night. There were a thousand, thousand bright stars shining over his head, and there was a little frost out, which left the grass under his foot white and crisp.

He stood there for an hour, for two hours, for three hours, and the frost increased greatly, so that he heard the breaking of the *traneens* under his foot as often as he moved. He was thinking, in his own mind, at last, that the *sheehogues* would not come that night. It was as good for him to return back again, when he heard a sound far away from him, coming towards him, and he recognized what it was at the first moment. The sound increased, and at first it was like the beating of waves on a stony shore, and then it was like the falling of a great waterfall, and at last it was like a loud storm in the tops of the trees, and then the whirlwind burst into the *rath* of one rout, and the *sheehogues* were in it.

It all went by him so suddenly that he lost his breath with it, but he came to himself on the spot, and put an ear on himself, listening to what they would say.

Scarcely had they gathered into the *rath* till they all began shouting, and screaming, and talking amongst themselves. Then each one of them cried out, "My horse, and bridle, and saddle! My horse, and bridle, and saddle!"

Guleesh took courage, and called out as loudly as any of them. "My horse, and bridle, and saddle! My horse, and bridle, and saddle!"

But before the word was well out of his mouth, another man cried out, "Oro! Guleesh, my boy, are you here with us again? How are you getting on with your woman? There's no use in your calling for your horse tonight. I'll go bail you won't play such a trick on us again. It was a good trick you played on us last year?"

"It was," said another man. "He won't do it again."

"Isn't he a prime lad, the same lad! To take a woman with him that never said as much to him as, 'How do you do?' since this time last year!" says the third man.

"Perhaps he likes to be looking at her," said another voice.

"And if the *omadawn* only knew that there's an herb growing up by his own door, and if he were to boil it and give it to her, she'd be well," said another voice.

"That's true for you."

"He is an *omadawn*."

"Don't bother your head with him; we'll be going."

"We'll leave the *bodach* as he is."

With that they rose up into the air, and out with them with one roolya-boolya the way they came; and they left poor Guleesh standing where they found him, and the two eyes going out of his head, looking after them and wondering.

He did not stand long till he returned back, and he thinking in his own mind on all he saw and heard, and wondering whether there was really an herb at his own door that would bring back the talk to the king's daughter. "It can't be," says he to himself, "that they would tell it to me, if there was any virtue in it. But perhaps the sheehogue didn't observe himself when he let the word slip out of his mouth. I'll search well as soon as the sun rises, whether there's any plant growing beside the house except thistles and dockings."

He went home, and as tired as he was he did not sleep a wink until the sun rose on the morrow. He got up then, and it was the first thing he did to go out and search well through the grass round about the house, trying could he get any herb that he did not recognize. And, indeed, he was not long searching till he observed a large strange herb that was growing up just by the gable of the house.

He went over to it, and observed it closely, and saw that

there were seven little branches coming out of the stalk, and seven leaves growing on every branch of them, and that there was a white sap in the leaves. "It's very wonderful," said he to himself, "that I never noticed this herb before. If there's any virtue in an herb at all, it ought to be in such a strange one as this."

He drew out his knife, cut the plant, and carried it into his own house, stripped the leaves off it and cut up the stalk. There came a thick, white juice out of it, as there comes out of the sow-thistle when it is bruised, except that the juice was more like oil.

He put it in a little pot and a little water in it, and laid it on the fire until the water was boiling. Then he took a cup, filled it half up with the juice, and put it to his own mouth. It came into his head then that perhaps it was poison that was in it, and that the good people were only tempting him that he might kill himself with that trick, or put the girl to death without meaning it. He put down the cup again, raised a couple of drops on the top of his finger, and put it to his mouth. It was not bitter, and indeed, had a sweet, agreeable taste. He grew bolder then, and drank the full of a thimble of it, and then as much again, and he never stopped till he had half the cup drunk. He fell asleep after that, and did not wake till it was night, and there was great hunger and great thirst on him.

He had to wait, then, till the day rose. But he determined, as soon as he should wake in the morning, that he would go to the king's daughter and give her a drink of the juice of the herb.

As soon as he got up in the morning, he went over to the priest's house with the drink in his hand, and he never felt himself so bold and valiant, and spirited and light, as he was that day. He was quite certain that it was the drink he drank which made him so hearty.

When he came to the house, he found the priest and the young lady within, and they were wondering greatly why he had not visited them for two days. He told them all his news, and said that he was certain that there was great power in that herb, and that it would do the lady no hurt, for he tried it himself and got good from it, and then he made her taste it, for he vowed and swore that there was no harm in it.

Guleesh handed her the cup, and she drank half of it, and then fell back on her bed and a heavy sleep came on her, and she never woke out of that sleep till the day on the morrow.

Guleesh and the priest sat up the entire night with her, waiting till she should awake, and they between hope and un-hope, between expectation of saving her and fear of hurting her.

She awoke at last when the sun had gone half its way through the heavens. She rubbed her eyes and looked like a person who did not know where she was. She was like one astonished when she saw Guleesh and the priest in the same room with her, and she sat up doing her best to collect her thoughts.

The two men were in great anxiety waiting to see would she speak, or would she not speak, and when they remained silent for a couple of minutes, the priest said to her, "Did you sleep well, Mary?"

And she answered him. "I slept, thank you."

No sooner did Guleesh hear her talking than he put a shout of joy out of him, and ran over to her and fell on his two knees. "A thousand thanks to God, who has given you back the talk. Lady of my heart, speak again to me."

The lady answered him that she understood it was he who boiled that drink for her, and gave it to her. That she was obliged to him from her heart for all the kindness he showed her since the day she first came to Ireland, and that he might be certain that she never would forget it.

Guleesh was ready to die with satisfaction and delight. Then they brought her food, and she ate with a good appetite, and was merry and joyous, and never left off talking with the priest while she was eating.

After that Guleesh went home to his house, and stretched himself on the bed and fell asleep again, for the force of the herb was not all spent, and he passed another day and a night sleeping. When he woke up he went back to the priest's house, and found that the young lady was in the same state, and that she was asleep almost since the time that he left the house.

He went into her chamber with the priest, and they remained watching beside her till she awoke the second time, and she had her talk as well as ever, and Guleesh was greatly rejoiced. The priest put food on the table again, and they ate together, and Guleesh used after that to come to the house from day to day, and the friendship that was between him and the king's daughter increased, because she had no one to speak to except Guleesh and the priest, and she liked Guleesh best.

So they married one another, and that was the fine wedding they had, and if I were to be there then, I would not be here now. But I heard it from a *birdeen* that there was neither cark nor care, sickness nor sorrow, mishap nor misfortune on them till the hour of their death. May the same be with me, and with us all!

21.

THE STORY OF
ETAIN AND MIDIR

ONCE UPON a time there was a High King of the Milesian race in Ireland named Eochy Airem, whose power and splendor were very great. All the sub-Kings, namely, Conor of Ulster, and Mesgedra of Leinster, and Curoi of Munster, and Ailill and Maev of Connacht, were obedient to him. But he was without a wife, and for this reason the sub-Kings and Princes of Ireland would not come to his festivals at Tara.

"For," said they, "there is no noble in Ireland who is a wifeless man, and a King is no king without a queen." And they would not bring their own wives to Tara without a queen there to welcome them, nor would they come themselves and leave their womenfolk at home.

So Eochy bade search be made through all the boundaries of Ireland for a maiden meet to be wife of the High King. And in time his messengers came back and said that they had found in Ulster, by the Bay of Cichmany, the fairest and most accomplished maiden in Ireland, and her name was Etain, daughter of Etar, lord of the territory called Echrad. So Eochy, when he had heard their report, went forth to woo the maiden.

When he drew near his journey's end he passed by a

certain spring of pure water where it chanced that Etain and her maids had come down that she might wash her hair. She held in her hand a comb of silver inlaid with gold, and before her was a *bason* of silver chased with figures of birds, and around the rim of it red carbuncles were set. Her mantle was purple with a fringe of silver, and it was fastened with a broad golden brooch. She wore also a tunic of green silk, stiff with embroidery of gold that glittered in the sun. Her hair before she loosed it was done in two mighty tresses, yellow like the flower of the water flag, each tress being plaited in four strands, and at the end of each strand a little golden ball. When she laid aside her mantle her arms came through the armholes of her tunic, white as the snow of a single night, and her cheeks were ruddy as the foxglove. Even and small were her teeth, as if a shower of pearls had fallen in her mouth. Her eyes were hyacinth-blue, her lips scarlet as the rowan-berry, her shoulders round and white, her fingers were long and her nails smooth and pink. Her feet also were slim, and white as sea-foam. The radiance of the moon was in her face, pride in her brows, and the light of wooing in her eyes. Of her it was said that there was no beauty among women compared with Etain's beauty, no sweetness compared with the sweetness of Etain.

When the King saw her his heart burned with love for her, and when he had speech with her he besought her to be his bride.

And she consented to that, and said, "Many have wooed me, O King, but I would none of them, for since I was a little child I have loved thee, for the high tales that I heard of thee and of thy glory."

Eochy replied, "Thine alone will I be if thou wilt have me."

So the King paid a great bride-price for her, and bore her away to Tara, and there they were wedded, and all men welcomed and honored the Queen.

Nor had she dwelt long in Tara before the enchantment of her beauty and her grace had worked upon the hearts of all about her, so that the man to whom she spoke grew pale at the womanly sweetness of her voice, and felt himself a king for that day. All fair things and bright she loved, such as racing steeds and shining raiment, and the sight of Eochy's warriors with their silken banners and shields decorated with rich ornament in red and blue. And she would have all about her happy and joyous, and she gave freely of her treasure, and of her smiles and loving words, if she might see the light of joy on the faces of men. But from pain or sadness that might not be cured she would turn away. In one thing only was sadness endurable to her and that was in her music, for when she sang or touched the harp all hearts were pierced with longing for they knew not what, and all eyes shed tears save hers alone, who looked as though she beheld, far from earth, some land more fair than words of man can tell. All the wonder of that land and all its immeasurable distance were in her song.

Now, Eochy the King had a brother whose name was Ailill Anglounach, or Ailill of the Single Stain, for one dark spot only was on his life, and it is of this that the story now shall tell. One day, when he had come from his own *Dún* to the yearly Assembly in the great Hall of Tara, he ate not at the banquet but gazed as it were at something afar off.

His wife said to him, "Why dost thou gaze so, Ailill? So do men look who are smitten with love."

Ailill was wroth with himself and turned his eyes away, but he said nothing, for that on which he gazed was the face of Etain.

After that Assembly was over, Ailill knew that the torment of love had seized him for his brother's wife, and he was sorely shamed and wrathful. The secret strife in his mind between his honor and the fierce and pitiless love that possessed him brought him into a sore sickness. And he went home to his *Dún* in Tethba and there lay ill for a year. Then Eochy the King went to see him, and came near him and laid his hand on his breast, and Ailill heaved a bitter sigh.

Eochy asked, "Why art thou not better of this sickness; how goes it with thee, now?"

"By my word," said Ailill. "No better, but worse each day and night."

"What ails thee, then?"

"Verily, I know not."

Then Eochy bade summon his chief physician, who might discover the cause of his brother's malady, for Ailill was wasting to death.

So, Fachtna the chief physician came and he laid his hand upon Ailill, and Ailill sighed. Then Fachtna said, "This is no bodily disease, but either Ailill suffers from the pangs of envy or from the torment of love." But Ailill was full of shame and he would not tell what ailed him, and Fachtna went away.

After this the time came that Eochy the High King should make a royal progress throughout his realm of Ireland, but Etain he left behind at Tara.

Before he departed he charged her saying, "Do thou be gentle and kind to my brother Ailill while he lives, and should he die, let his burial mound be heaped over him, and a pillar stone set up above it, and his name written thereon in letters of Ogham." Then the King took leave of Ailill and looked to see him again on earth no more.

After a while Etain bethought her and said, "Let us go to see how it fares with Ailill."

So she went to where he lay in his *Dún* at Tethba. And seeing him wasted and pale she was moved with pity and distress.

"What ails thee, young man? Long thou hast lain prostrate, in fair weather and in foul, thou who wert wont to be so swift and strong?"

And Ailill said, "Truly, I have a cause for my suffering. I cannot eat, nor listen to the music makers. My affliction is very sore."

Then said Etain, "Though I am a woman I am wise in many a thing. Tell me what ails thee and thy healing shall be done."

Ailill replied, "Blessing be with thee, oh fair one; I am not worthy of thy speech. I am torn by the contention of body and of soul."

Then Etain deemed that she knew somewhat of his trouble. "If thy heart is set on any of the white maidens that are my handmaids, tell me of it, and I shall court her for thee and she shall come to thee."

Ailill cried out, "Love indeed, oh Queen, hath brought me low. It is a plague nearer than the skin, it overwhelms my soul as an earthquake. It is farther than the height of the sky, and harder to win than the treasures of the Faery Folk. If I contend with it, it is like a combat with a specter. If I fly to the ends of the earth from it, it is there. If I seek to seize it, it is a passion for an echo. It is thou, oh my love, who hast brought me to this, and thou alone canst heal me, or I shall never rise again."

Then Etain went away and left him. But still in her palace in Tara she was haunted by his passion and his misery, and though she loved him not, she could not endure his pain, nor the triumph of grim death over his youth and beauty.

So at last she went to him again. "If it lies with me, Ailill, to heal thee of thy sickness, I may not let thee die." She made a tryst to meet him on the morrow at a house of Ailill's between *Dún* Tethba and Tara. "But be it not at Tara," she said. "For that is the palace of the High King."

All that night Ailill lay awake with the thought of his tryst with Etain. But on the morrow morn a heaviness came upon his eyelids, and a druid sleep overcame him. There all day he lay buried in slumbers from which none could wake him, until the time of his meeting with Etain was overpast.

But Etain, when she had come to the place of the tryst, looked out, and behold, a youth having the appearance and the garb of Ailill was approaching from Tethba. He entered the bower where she was, but no lover did she there meet. Only a sick and sorrowful man who spake coldly to her and lamented the sufferings of his malady, and after a short time he went away.

Next day, Etain went to see Ailill and to hear how he did. And Ailill entreated her forgiveness that he had not kept his tryst.

"For," said he, "a druid slumber descended upon me, and I lay as one dead from morn till eve. It seems as if the strange passion that has befallen me were washed away in that slumber. Fr now, Etain, I love thee no more but as my Queen and my sister, and I am recovered as if from an evil dream."

Then Etain knew that powers not of earth were mingling in her fate, and she pondered much of these things, and grew less lighthearted than of old. When the King came back, he rejoiced to find his brother whole and sound and merry, as Ailill had ever been, and he praised Etain for her gentleness and care.

Now, after a time as Etain was by herself in her sunny bower she was aware of a man standing by her, whom she had never seen before. Young he was, and grey-eyed, with curling golden hair, and in his hand he bore two spears. His mantle was of crimson silk, his tunic of saffron, and a golden helmet was on his head.

And as she gazed upon him, "Etain," he said. "The time

is come for thee to return; we have missed thee and sorrowed for thee long enough in the Land of Youth."

Etain replied, "Of what land dost thou speak?"

Then he chanted to her a song:

> *"Come with me, Etain, O come away,*
> *To that oversea land of mine!*
> *Where music haunts the happy day,*
> *And rivers run with wine;*
> *Where folk are careless, and young, and gay,*
> *And none saith 'mine' or 'thine.'*
> *Golden curls on the proud young head,*
> *And pearls in the tender mouth;*
> *Manhood, womanhood, white and red,*
> *And love that grows not loth*
> *When all the world's desires are dead,*
> *And all the dreams of youth.*
> *Away from the cloud of Adam's sin!*
> *Away from grief and care!*
> *This flowery land thou dwellest in*
> *Seems rude to us, and bare;*
> *For the naked strand of the Happy Land*
> *Is twenty times as fair."*

When Etain heard this she stood motionless and as one that dreams awake, for it seemed to her as if she must follow that music whithersoever it went on earth or beyond the earth.

But at last remembrance came upon her and she said to the stranger, "Who art thou, that I, the High King's wife, should follow a nameless man and betray my troth?"

"Thy troth was due to me before it was due to him, and, moreover, were it not for me thou hadst broken it already. I am Midir the Proud, a prince among the people of Dana, and thy husband, Etain. Thus it was, that when I took thee to wife in the Land of Youth, the jealousy of thy rival, Fuamnach, was awakened. Having decoyed me from home by a false report, she changed thee by magical arts into a butterfly and then contrived a mighty tempest that drove thee abroad. Seven years wast thou borne hither and thither on the blast till chance blew thee into the faery palace of Angus my kinsman, by the waters of the Boyne. But Angus knew thee, for the Faery Folk may not disguise themselves from each other. He built for thee a magical sunny bower with open windows, through which thou might dwell, and about it were all manner of blossoming herbs and shrubs. On the odor and honey of these thou didst live and grow fair and well-nourished. But in the end Fuamnach got tidings of thee, and again the druid tempest descended and blew thee forth for another seven years of wandering and woe. Then it chanced that thou wert blown through the roof window of the *Dún* of Etar by the Bay of Cichmany, and fell into the goblet from which his wife was drinking, and thee she drank down with that draught of ale. And in due time thou wast born again in the guise of a mortal maid and daughter to Etar the Warrior. But thou art no mortal, nor of mortal kin, for it is one thousand and twelve years from the time when thou wast born in Faery Land till Etar's wife bore thee as a child on earth."

Etain was bewildered, and her mind ran back on many a half-forgotten thing. She gazed as into a gulf of visions, full of dim shapes, strange and glorious. And Midir, as she looked at him again seemed transfigured, taller and mightier than before, and a light flame flickered from his helmet's crest and moved like wings about his shoulders.

At last she said, "I know not what thou sayest if it be truth or not, but this I know: that I am the wife of the High King and I will not break my troth."

"It were broken already," answered Midir. "But for me, for I it was who laid a druidic sleep on Ailill, and it was I who came to thee in his shape that thy honor might not be stained."

Etain said, "I learned then that honor is more than life."

"But if Eochy the High King consent to let thee go, wilt thou then come with me to my land and thine?"

"In that case," said Etain, "I will go."

And the time went by, and Etain abode in Tara. The High King did justice and made war and held the great Assembly as he was used. But one day in summer Eochy arose very early to breathe the morning air. He stood by himself leaning on the rampart of his great *Dún*, and looking over the flowery plain of Bregia. And as he thus gazed he was aware of a young warrior standing by his side. Grey-eyed the youth was, and golden-haired, and he was splendidly armed and appareled as beseemed the lord of a great clan of the Gael. Eochy bade him welcome courteously, and asked him of the cause of his coming.

"I am come," he said, "to play a game of chess with thee, O King. For thou art renowned for thy skill in that game, and to test that skill am I come. And my name is Midir, of the People of Dana, whom they have called The Proud."

"Willingly," replied the King. "But I have here no chessboard, and mine is in the chamber where the Queen is sleeping."

"That is easily remedied," said Midir, and he drew from his cloak a folding chessboard whose squares were alternate gold and silver. From a men-bag made of brazen chain work he drew out a set of men adorned with flashing jewels, and he set them in array.

"I will not play," then said Eochy, "unless we play for a stake."

"For what stake shall we play, then?" asked Midir.

"I care not. But do thou perform tasks for me if I win, and I shall bestow of my treasures upon thee if I lose."

So they played a game, and Eochy won. Then Eochy bade Midir clear the plains of Meath about Tara from rocks and stones, and Midir brought at night a great host of the Faery Folk, and it was done. And again he played with Eochy, and again he lost, and this time he cut down the forest of Breg. The third time Midir lost again, and his task was to build a causeway across the moor of Lamrach.

Now, at night, while Midir and the faery host were laboring at the causeway and their oxen drawing to it innumerable loads of earth and gravel, the steward of Eochy stole out and hid himself to watch them, for it was a prohibition to see them at work. And he observed that the faery oxen were not harnessed with a thong across their foreheads, that the pull might be upon their brows and necks, as was the manner with the Gael, but with yokes upon their shoulders. This he reported to Eochy, who found it good, and he ordered that henceforth the children of the Gael should harness their plough-oxen with the yoke upon their shoulders, and so it was done from that day forth. Hence Eochy got his name of Airem, or "The Ploughman," for he was the first of the Gael to put the yoke upon the shoulder of the ox.

But it was said that because the Faery Folk were watched as they made that noble causeway, there came a breach in it at one place which none could ever rightly mend.

When all their works were accomplished, Midir came again to Eochy, and this time he bore a dark and fierce countenance and was high girt as for war.

The King welcomed him, and Midir said, "Thou hast treated me hardly and put slavish tasks upon me. All that seemed good to thee have I done, but now I am moved with anger against thee."

"I return not anger for anger," said Eochy. "Say what satisfaction I can make thee."

"Let us once more play at chess," said Midir.

"Good. What stake wilt thou have now?"

"The stake to be whatever the winner shall demand."

Then they played for the fourth time and Eochy lost. "Thou hast won the game," said he.

"I had won long ago had I chosen."

"What dost thou demand of me?" asked Eochy.

"To hold Etain in my arms and obtain a kiss from her," replied Midir.

The King was silent for a while and after that he said, "Come back in one month from this day and the stake which I have lost shall be paid."

But Eochy summoned together all the host of the heroes of the Gael, and they surrounded Tara, ring within ring. The King himself and Etain were in the palace, with the outer court of it shut and locked. For they looked that Midir should come with a great host of the Danaan folk to carry off the Queen. And on the appointed day, as the kings sat at meat, Etain and her handmaids were dispensing the wine to them as was wont. Then suddenly as they feasted and talked, behold, Midir, stood in the midst of them. If he was fair and noble to look on as he had appeared before to the King and to Etain, he was fairer now, for the splendor of the Immortals clothed him, and his jewels flamed as he moved like eyes of living light. And all the kings and lords and champions who were present gazed on him in amazement and were silent, as the King arose and gave him welcome.

"Thou hast received me as I expected to be received," said Midir, "and now let thy debt be paid, since I for my part faithfully performed all that I undertook."

"I must consider the matter yet longer," said Eochy.

"Thou hast promised Etain's very self to me. That is

what hath come from thee."

And when she heard that word, Etain blushed for shame.

"Blush not," said Midir. "For all the treasures of the Land of Youth have not availed to win thee from Eochy, and it is not of thine own will that thou art won, but because the time is come to return to thy kin."

Then said Eochy, "I have not promised Etain's self to thee, but to take her in thine arms and kiss her, and now do so if thou wilt."

Then Midir took his weapons in his left hand and placed his right around Etain. When he did so they rose up in the air over the heads of the host, and passed through a roof window in the palace. Then all rose up, tumultuous and angry, and rushed out of doors, but nothing could they see save two white swans that circled high in air around the Hill of Tara, and then flew southwards and away towards the faery mountain of Slievenamon. And thus Etain the immortal rejoined the Immortals. But a daughter of Etain and of Eochy, who was another Etain in name and in beauty, became in due time a wife, and mother of kings.

22.

THE CHASE OF THE GILLA DACAR

IN THE REIGN of Cormac mac Art, grandson of Conn of the Hundred Battles, the order of precedence and dignity in the court of the High King at Tara was as follows. First came great Cormac, the kingly, the hospitable, warrior and poet, and he was supreme over all. Next in order came the five kings of the five Provinces of Ireland, namely, Ulster, Munster, Connacht, Leinster, and Mid-Erin. After these ranked the captains of the royal host, of whom Finn, son of Cuill, was the chief.

Now the privileges of the Fianna of Erin were many and great. To wit, in every county in Ireland one townland, and in every townland a *cartron* of land, and in the house of every gentleman the right to have a young deer-hound or a beagle kept at nurse from November to May, together with many other taxes and royalties not to be recounted here. But if they had these many and great privileges, yet greater than these were the toils and hardships which they had to endure. In guarding the coasts of all Ireland from oversea invaders and marauders, and in keeping down all robbers and outlaws and evil folk within the kingdom, for this was the duty laid upon them by their bond of service to the King.

Now the summer half of the year was wont to be ended by a great hunting in one of the forests of Ireland, and so it was that one Allhallowtide, when the great banquet of Finn in his *Dún* on the Hill of Allen was going forward, and the hall resounded with cheerful talk and laughter and with the music of *tympan* and of harp, Finn asked of the assembled captains in what part of Erin they should proceed to beat up game on the morrow. It was agreed among them to repair to the territory of Thomond and Desmond in Munster, and from Allen they set out accordingly and came to the Hill of Knockany.

Thence they threw out the hunt and sent their bands of beaters through many a gloomy ravine and by many a rugged hill pass and many a fair open plain. Desmond's high hills, called now Slievelogher, they beat, and the smooth, swelling hills of Slievenamuck, and the green slopes of grassy Slievenamon, and the towering rough crags of the Decies, and thence on to the dark woods of Belachgowran.

While the great hunt was going forward, Finn with certain of his chief captains sat on a high mound to overlook it. There, with Finn, were Goll and Art mac Morna, and Liagan the swift runner, and Dermot of the Love Spot, and Keelta, son of Ronan. There also was Conan the Bald, the man of scurrilous tongue, and a score or so more. Sweet it was to Finn and his companions to hear from the woods and wildernesses around them the many-tongued baying of the hounds and the cries and whistling of the beaters, the shouting of the strong men and the notes of the Fian hunting-horn.

When they had sat there awhile one of Finn's men came running quickly towards him and said, "A stranger is approaching us from the westward, oh Finn, and I much mislike his aspect."

With that all the Fians looked up and beheld upon the
hillside a huge man, looking like some Fomorian marauder,
black-visaged and ugly, with a sour countenance and
ungainly limbs. On his back hung a dingy black shield, on
his misshapen left thigh he wore a sharp broad-bladed
sword, and projecting over his shoulder were two long
lances with broad rusty heads. He wore garments that
looked as if they had been buried in a cinder heap, and a
loose ragged mantle. Behind him there shambled a sulky,
ill-shapen mare with a bony *carcase* and bowed knees, and
on her neck a clumsy iron halter. With a rope her master
hauled her along, with violent jerks that seemed as if they
would wrench her head from her scraggy neck. Ever and
anon the mare would stand and jib, when the man laid on
her ribs such blows from a strong iron-shod cudgel that
they sounded like the surges of the sea beating on a rocky
coast. Short as was the distance from where the man and
his horse were first perceived to where Finn was standing,
it was long ere they traversed it. At last, however, he came
into the presence of Finn and louted before him, doing
obeisance. Finn lifted his hand over him and bade him
speak, and declare his business and his name and rank.

"I know not," said the fellow, "of what blood I am,
gentle or simple, but only this, that I am a *wight* from
oversea looking for service and wages. And as I have heard
of thee, oh Finn, that thou art not wont to refuse any man,
I came to take service with thee if thou wilt have me."

"Neither shall I refuse thee," answered Finn. "But what
brings thee here with a horse and no horseboy?"

"Good enough reason," said the stranger. "I have
much ado to get meat for my own belly, seeing that I eat
for a hundred men. I will not have any horseboy meddling
with my ration."

"What name dost thou bear?"

"I am called the Gilla Dacar, the Hard Gillie," replied he.

"Why was that name given thee?"

"Good enough reason for that also," spake the stranger. "For of all the lads in the world there is none harder than I am for a lord to get any service and obedience from." Then turning to Conan the Bald he said, "Whether among the Fianna is a horseman's pay or a footman's the highest?"

"A horseman's, surely," said Conan, "seeing that he gets twice the pay of a footman."

"Then I am a horseman in thy service, Finn," said the gillie. "I call thee to observe that I have here a horse, and moreover that as a horseman I came among the Fianna. Have I thy authority," he went on, "to turn out my steed among thine?"

"Turn her out," quoth Finn.

The big man flung his mare the rope and immediately she galloped off to where the Fian horses were grazing. Here she fell to biting and kicking them, knocking out the eye of one and snapping off another's ear and breaking the leg of another with a kick.

"Take away thy mare, big man!" cried Conan. "Or by Heaven and Earth were it not that Finn told thee to let her loose I would let loose her brains. Many a bad bargain has Finn made but never a worse than thou."

"By Heaven and Earth," said the gillie. "That I never will, for I have no horseboy, and I will do no horseboy's work."

Conan mac Morna took the iron halter and laid it on the stranger's horse and brought the beast back to Finn and held it there.

Said Finn to Conan, "I have never seen thee do horseboy's service even to far better men than this gillie.

How now if thou wert to leap on the brute's back and gallop her to death over hill and dale in payment for the mischief she hath wrought among our steeds?"

At this word Conan clambered up on the back of the big man's mare, and with all his might he smote his two heels into her, but the mare never stirred.

"I perceive what ails her," said Finn. "She will never stir till she has a weight of men on her equal to that of her own rider."

Then thirteen men of the Fianna scrambled up laughing behind Conan, and the mare lay down under them, and then got up again, they still clinging to her.

At this the big man said, "It appears that you are making a sport and mockery of my mare, and that even I myself do not escape from it. It is well for me that I have not spent the rest of the year in your company, seeing what a jest ye have made of me the very first day. And I perceive, Oh, Finn, that thou art very unlike the report that is made of thee. And now I bid thee farewell, for of thy service I have had enough."

So with downcast head and despondent looks the big gillie shambled slowly away until he had passed out of view of the Fianna, behind the shoulder of the hill. Having arrived here he tucked up his coat to his waist, and fast though be the flight of the swallow, and fast that of the roe-deer, and fast the rush of a roaring wind over a mountain top in mid-March, no faster are these than the bounding speed and furious flight of the big man down the hillside toward the West.

No sooner did the mare see that her master had departed than she too dashed uncontrollably forward and flew down the hillside after him. And as the Fians saw Conan the Bald and his thirteen companions thus carried off, willy-nilly, they broke into a roar of laughter and ran alongside mocking them. But Conan, seeing that they were being carried off in the wake of the big man of evil aspect, of whom none knew whence or who he was, he was terrified and began reviling and cursing.

He shouted to Finn, "A palsy seize thee, Finn. May some rascally churl, that is if possible of worse blood than thyself, have thy head, unless thou follow and rescue us wheresoever this monster shall bring us."

So Finn and the Fianna ran, and the mare ran, over bare hills and by deep glens, till at last they came to Corcaguiny in Kerry, where the gillie set his face to the blue ocean, and the mare dashed in after him. But ere he did so, Liagan the Swift got two hands on the tail of the mare, though further he could not win. He was towed in, still clinging to his hold, and over the rolling billows away they went, the fourteen Fians on the wild mare's back, and Liagan haled along by her tail.

"What is to be done now?" asked Oisín of Finn when they had arrived at the beach.

"Our men are to be rescued," said Finn. "For to that we are bound by the honor of the Fianna. Whithersoever they are gone; thither must we follow and win them back by fair means or foul. But to that end we must first fit out a galley."

So, in the end it was agreed that Finn and fourteen men of his bravest and best champions should sail oversea in search of the Gilla Dacar and his captives, while Oisín remained in Erin and exercised rule over the Fianna in the place of his father.

After a while, then, a swift galley was made ready by Finn and stored with victual, and with arms, and also with gold and raiment to make gifts withal if need should be. And into the ship came the fifteen valiant men, and gripped their oars while Finn steered. Soon the sea whitened around their oar blades, and over the restless, rolling masses of the many-hued and voiceful billows, the ship clove her way to the West. And the Fians, who were wont to be wakened by the twittering of birds over their hunting booths in the greenwood, now delighted to hear, day after day as they roused themselves at morn, the lapping of the wide waters of the world against their vessel's bows, or the thunder of pounding surges when the wind blew hard.

At length after many days the sharpest-eyed of the men of Finn saw far off what seemed a mountain rising from the sea, and to it they shaped their course. When they had come to that land they found themselves under the shadow of a great grey cliff, and beneath it slippery rocks covered with seaweed.

Dermot, who was the most active of the company, was bidden to mount the cliff and to procure means of drawing up the rest of the party. But of what land might lie on the top of that wall of rock none of them could discover anything. Dermot, descending from the ship, then climbed with difficulty up the face of the cliff, while the others made fast their ship among the rocks. But Dermot having arrived at the top saw no habitation of man, and could compass no way of helping his companions to mount. He went therefore boldly forward into the unknown land, hoping to obtain some help, if any friendly and hospitable folk could there be found.

Before he had gone far he came into a wild wood, thick and tangled, and full of the noise of streams, and the sough of winds, and twittering of birds, and hum of bees. After he had traversed this wilderness for a while he came to a mighty tree with densely interwoven branches, and beneath it a pile of rocks, having on its summit a pointed drinking horn wreathed with rich ornament, and at its foot a well of pure bright water. Dermot, being now thirsty, took the horn and would have filled it at the well, but as he stooped down to do so he heard a loud, threatening murmur which seemed to rise from it.

"I perceive," he said to himself, "that I am forbidden to drink from this well."

Nevertheless thirst compelled him, and he drank his fill. In no long time thereafter he saw an armed warrior of hostile aspect coming towards him through the wood. No courteous greeting did he give to Dermot, but began to revile him for roaming in his wood and wilderness, and for drinking his water.

Thereupon they fought, and for the rest of the afternoon they took and gave hard blows neither subduing the other, till at last as darkness began to fall the warrior suddenly dived into the well and was seen no more.

Dermot, vexed at this ending of the combat, then made him ready to spend the night in that place, but first he slew a deer in the wood, made a fire, whereat he roasted pieces of the deer's flesh on spits of white hazel, and drank abundantly of the well-water, and then slept soundly through the night.

Next morning when he awakened and went to the well he found the Champion of the Well standing there and awaiting him.

"It is not enough, Dermot," said he angrily, "for thee to traverse my woods at will and to drink my water, but thou must even also slay my deer."

Then they closed in combat again, and dealt each other blow for blow and wound for wound till evening parted them, and the champion dived into the well as before.

On the third day it went even so. But as evening came on Dermot, watching closely, rushed at the champion just as he was about to plunge into the well, and gripped him in his arms. But nonetheless the Champion of the Well made his, dive, and took down Dermot with him. And a darkness and faintness came over Dermot, but when he awoke, he found himself in a wide, open country, flowery and fair, and before him the walls and towers of a royal city. Thither the champion, sorely wounded, was now borne off, while a crowd of his people came round Dermot, and beat and wounded him, leaving him on the ground for dead.

After night had fallen, when all the people of the city in the Land Undersea had departed, a stalwart champion, well-armed and of bold appearance, came upon Dermot and stirred him with his foot. Dermot thereon awoke from his swoon and, warrior-like, reached out his hand for his arms.

But the champion said, "Wait awhile, my son, I have not come to do thee hurt or harm. Thou hast chosen an ill place to rest and slumber in, before the city of thine enemy. Rise and follow me, and I shall bestow thee far better than that."

Dermot then rose and followed the champion, and long and far they journeyed until they came to a high-towered fortress, wherein were thrice fifty valiant men-at-arms and fair women. The daughter of that champion, a white-toothed, rosy-cheeked, smooth-handed, and black-eyebrowed maid, received Dermot, kindly and welcomefully, and applied healing herbs to his wounds, and in no long time he was made as good a man as ever. And thus he remained, and was entertained most royally with the best of viands and of liquors. The first part of every night those in that *Dún* were wont to spend in feasting, and the second in recreation and entertainment of the mind, with music and with poetry and bardic tales, and the third part in sound and healthful slumber, till the sun in his fiery journey rose over the heavy-clodded earth on the morrow morn.

The King of that country, who was the champion that had aroused Dermot, told him this was the land of Sorca, and that he had showed this kindness to Dermot for that he himself had once been on wage and service with Finn, son of Cuill. "And a better master," said he, "man never had."

Now, the story turns to tell of what befell Finn and the remainder of his companions when Dermot left them in the ship. After a while, seeing that he did not return, and being assured that some mischief or hindrance must have befallen him, they made an attempt to climb the cliff after him, having noted which way he went. With much toil and peril they accomplished this, and then journeying forward and following on Dermot's track, they came at last to the well in the wild wood. They saw near by the remains of the deer and the ashes of the fire that Dermot had kindled to cook it. But from this place they could discover no track of his going. While they were debating on what should next be done, they saw riding towards them a tall warrior on a dark grey horse with a golden bridle, who greeted them courteously. From him they enquired as to whether he had seen aught of their companion, Dermot, in the wilderness.

"Follow me," said the warrior, "and you shall shortly have tidings of him."

They followed the strange horseman into the forest by many dark and winding ways, until at last they came into a rocky ravine, where they found the mouth of a great cavern opening into the hillside. Into this they went, and the way led them downward until it seemed as if they were going into the bowels of the earth. At last the light began to shine round them, and they came out into a lovely land of flowery plains and green woods and singing streams. In no long time thereafter they came to a great royal *Dún*, where he who led them was hailed as king and lord, and here, to their joy, they found their comrade, Dermot of the Love Spot, who told them of all his adventures and heard from them of theirs.

This ended, and when they had been entertained and refreshed, the lord of that place spoke to Finn and said, "I have now, O Finn, within my fortress, the fifteen stoutest heroes that the world holds. To this end have I brought you here, that ye might make war with me upon mine enemy the Champion of the Well, who is king of the land bordering on mine. He ceases not to persecute and to harry my people because, in his arrogance, he would have all the Under World country subject to himself alone. Say now if ye will embrace this enterprise and help me to defend my own: and if not I shall set you again upon the land of Erin."

Finn replied, "What of my fifteen men that were carried away on the wild mare's back oversea?"

"They are guarding the marches of my kingdom," said the King of Sorca, "and all is well with them and shall be well."

Finn agreed to take service with the King of Sorca, and next day they arrayed themselves for fight and went out at the head of the host. Ere long they came upon the army of the King of the Well, and with him was the King of the Greeks and a band of fierce mercenaries. Also was the daughter of the Greek King, by name Tasha of the White Side, a maiden who in beauty and grace surpassed all other women of the world, as the Shannon surpasses all rivers of Erin and the eagle surpasses all birds of the air. Now, the stories of Finn and his generosity and great deeds had reached her since she was a child, and she had set her love on him, though she had never seen his face till now.

When the hosts were met, the King of the Greeks said, "Who of my men will stand forth and challenge the best of these men of Erin to single combat, that their metal may be proved? For to us it is unknown what manner of men they be."

The son of the King of the Greeks said, "I will go."

So, on the side of Finn, Oscar, son of Oisín, was chosen to match the son of the Greek King, and the two hosts sat down peacefully together to watch the weapon-play. And Tasha the princess sat by Finn, son of Cuill.

Oscar and the King's son stepped into their fighting place, and fierce was the combat that arose between them, as when two roaring surges of the sea dash against each other in a fissure of the rocks, and the spray-cloud bursts from them high into the air. Long they fought, and many red wounds did each of them give and receive, till at last Oscar beat the Greek prince to the earth and smote off his head. Then one host groaned for woe and discouragement, while the other shouted for joy of victory, and so they parted for the night, each to their own camp.

And in the camp of the folk of Sorca they found Conan the Bald, and the fourteen men that had gone with him on the mare's back.

But when night had fallen, Tasha stole from the wizard of the Greek King his branch of silver bells that when shaken would lay asleep a host of men, and with the aid of this she passed from the camp of the Greeks, and through the sentinels, and came to the tent of Finn.

On the morrow morn the King of the Greeks found that his daughter had fled to be the wife of Finn, son of Cuill, and he offered a mighty reward to whosoever would slay Finn and bring Tasha back.

But when the two armies closed in combat the Fians and the host of the King of Sorca charged so fiercely home, that they drove their foes before them as a winter gale drives before it a cloud of madly whirling leaves. Those that were not slain in the fight and the pursuit went to their own lands and abode there in peace, and thus was the war ended of the King of Sorca and the Lord of the Well.

Then the King of Sorca had Finn and his comrades before him and gave them praise and thanks for their valor.

"What reward," he asked, "will ye that I make you for the saving of the kingdom of Sorca?"

"Thou wert in my service awhile," said Finn. "And I mind not that I paid thee any wage for it. Let that service even go against this, and so we are quits."

"Nay, then!" cried Conan the Bald. "What shall I have for my ride on the mare of the Gilla Dacar?"

"What wilt thou have?" said the King of Sorca.

"This," answered Conan, "and nothing else will I accept. Let fourteen of the fairest women of the land of Sorca be put on that same mare, and thy wife, oh King, clinging to its tail. Let them be thus haled across the sea until they come to Corcaguiny in the land of Erin. I will have none of thy gold and silver, but the indignity that has been put upon me doth demand an honorable satisfaction."

The King of Sorca smiled, and he said, "Behold thy men, Finn."

Finn turned his head to look round, and as he did so the plain and the encampment of the Faery Host vanished from his sight, and he saw himself standing on the shingly strand of a little bay, with rocky heights to right and left, crowned with yellow whin bushes whose perfume mingled with the salt sea wind. It was the spot where he had seen the Gilla Dacar and his mare take water on the coast of Kerry.

Finn stared over the sea, to discover, if he might, by what means he had come thither, but nothing could he see there save the sunlit water, and nothing hear but what seemed a low laughter from the twinkling ripples that broke at his feet.

Then he looked for his men, who stood there, dazed like himself and rubbing their eyes. There too stood the Princess Tasha, who stretched out her white arms to him. Finn went over and took her hands.

"Shoulder your spears, good lads!" he called to his men. "Follow me now to the Hill of Allen, and to the wedding feast of Tasha and of Finn mac Cuill."

23.

THE QUEST OF THE
SONS OF TURENN

LONG AGO, when the people of Dana yet held lordship in Erin, they were sorely afflicted by hordes of sea-rovers named Fomorians who used to harry the country and carry off youths and maidens into captivity. They also imposed cruel and extortionate taxes upon the people, for every kneading trough, and every quern for grinding corn, and every flagstone for baking bread had to pay its tax. And an ounce of gold was paid as a poll-tax for every man, and if any man would not or could not pay, his nose was cut off. Under this tyranny the whole country groaned, but they had none who was able to band them together and to lead them in battle against their oppressors.

Now before this it happened that one of the lords of the Danaans named Kian had married with Ethlinn, daughter of Balor, a princess of the Fomorians. They had a son named Lugh Lamfada, or Lugh of the Long Arm, who grew up into a youth of surpassing beauty and strength. And if his body was noble and mighty, no less so was his mind, for lordship and authority grew to him by the gift of the Immortals. Whatever he purposed that would he perform, whatever it might cost in time or toil, in tears or in blood. Now this Lugh was not brought up in Erin but in

a far-off isle of the western sea, where the sea-god
Mananan and the other Immortals nurtured and taught
him, and made him fit alike for warfare or for sovereignty,
when his day should come to work their will on earth.
Hither in due time came the report of the grievous and
dishonoring oppression wrought by the Fomorians upon
the people of Dana, and that report was heard by Lugh.

Lugh said to his tutors, "It were a worthy deed to
rescue my father and the people of Erin from this tyranny;
let me go thither and attempt it."

And they said to him, "Go, and blessing and victory be
with thee."

So Lugh armed himself and mounted his faery steed,
and called his friends and foster-brothers about him.
Across the bright and heaving surface of the waters they
rode like the wind, until they took land in Erin.

Now the chiefs of the Danaan folk were assembled
upon the Hill of Usnach, which is upon the western side of
Tara in Meath, in order to meet there the stewards of the
Fomorians and to pay them their tribute. As they awaited
the arrival of the Fomorians they became aware of a
company on horseback, coming from the west. Before
them rode a young man who seemed to command them all,
and whose countenance was as radiant as the sun upon a
dry summer's day, so that the Danaans could scarcely gaze
upon it. He rode upon a white horse and was armed with a
sword, and on his head was a helmet set with precious
stones. The Danaan folk welcomed him as he came among
them, and asked him of his name and his business among
them. As they were thus talking another band drew near,
numbering nine times nine persons, who were the stewards
of the Fomorians coming to demand their tribute. They
were men of a fierce and swarthy countenance, and as they

came haughtily and arrogantly forward, the Danaans all rose up to do them honor.

Then Lugh said, "Why do ye rise up before that grim and ill-looking band and not before us?"

Said the King of Erin, "We needs must do so, for if they saw but a child of a month old sitting down when they came near they would hold it cause enough to attack and slay us."

"I am greatly minded to slay them," said Lugh, and repeated it, "Very greatly minded."

"That would be bad for us," said the King, "for our death and destruction would surely follow."

"Ye are too long under oppression," said Lugh.

He gave the word for onset and he and his comrades rushed upon the Fomorians. In a moment the hillside rang with blows and with the shouting of warriors. In no long time all of the Fomorians were slain, save nine men, and these were taken alive and brought before Lugh.

"Ye also should be slain," said Lugh, "but that I am minded to send you as ambassadors to your King. Tell him that he may seek homage and tribute where he will henceforth, but Ireland will pay him none forever."

Then the Fomorians went northwards away, and the people of Dana made them ready for war. They made Lugh their captain and warlord, for the sight of his face heartened them, and made them strong. They marveled that they had endured their slavery so long.

In the meantime word was brought to Balor of the Mighty Blows, King of the Fomorians, and to his queen Kethlinn of the Twisted Teeth, of the shame and destruction that had been done to their stewards. They assembled a great host of the sea-rovers and manned their warships, and the Northern Sea was white with the foam of

their oar blades as they swept down upon the shores of
Erin.

Balor commanded them, saying, "When ye have utterly
destroyed and subdued the people of Dana, then make fast
your ships with cables to the land of Erin. Tow it here to
the north of us into the region of ice and snow, and it shall
trouble us no longer."

So the host of Balor took land by the Falls of Dara and
began plundering and devastating the province of
Connacht.

Then Lugh sent messengers abroad to bring his host
together. Among them was his own father, Kian, son of
Canta. As Kian went northwards on his errand to rouse the
Ulstermen, and was now come to the plain of Murthemny
near by Dundealga, he saw three warriors armed and riding
across the plain. Now these three were the sons of Turenn,
by name Brian and Iuchar and Iucharba. And there was an
ancient blood-feud between the house of Canta and the
house of Turenn, so that they never met without
bloodshed.

Then Kian thought to himself, "If my brothers Cu and
Kethan were here there might be a pretty fight, but as they
are three to one I would do better to fly." Now there was a
herd of wild swine nearby, and Kian changed himself by
druidic sorceries into a wild pig and fell to rooting up the
earth along with the others.

When the sons of Turenn came up to the herd, Brian
said, "Brothers, did ye see the warrior who just now was
journeying across the plain?"

"We saw him," said they.

"What is become of him?" asked Brian.

"Truly, we cannot tell," said the brothers.

"It is good watch ye keep in time of war!" said Brian.
"But I know what has taken him out of our sight. He

struck himself with a magic wand, and changed himself into the form of one of yonder swine, and he is rooting the earth among them now. Wherefore I deem that he is no friend to us."

"If so, we have no help for it," said they, "for the herd belongs to some man of the Danaans. Even if we set to and begin to kill the swine, the pig of druidism might be the very one to escape."

"Have ye learned so little in your place of studies," said Brian, "that ye cannot distinguish a druidic beast from a natural beast?" And with that he smote his two brothers with a magic wand, and changed them into two slender, fleet hounds, and they darted in among the herd. Then all the herd scattered and fled, but the hounds separated the druidic pig and chased it towards a wood where Brian awaited it. As it passed, Brian flung his spear, and it pierced the chest of the pig and brought it down.

The pig screamed, "Evil have you done to cast at me."

Brian said, "That hath the sound of human speech!"

"I am in truth a man," said the pig. "I am Kian, son of Canta, and I pray you show me mercy."

"That will we," said Iuchar and Iucharba, "and sorry are we for what has happened."

"Nay," said Brian. "I swear by the Wind and the Sun that if thou hadst seven lives I would take them all."

"Grant me a favor then," pleaded Kian.

"We shall grant it," said Brian.

"Let me return into my own form that I may die in the shape of a man."

"I had *liefer* kill a man than a pig," said Brian.

Then Kian became a man again and stood before them, the blood trickling from his breast. "I have outwitted you, now!" cried he. "For if ye had killed a pig ye would have paid a pig's *eric,* but now ye shall pay the *eric* of a man.

Never was greater *eric* in the land of Erin than that which ye shall pay, and I swear that the very weapons with which ye slay me shall tell the tale to the avenger of blood."

"Then you shall be slain with no weapons at all," said Brian. They picked up the stones on the Plain of Murthemny and rained them upon him till he was all one wound, and he died. So they buried him as deep as the height of a man, and went their way to join the host of Lugh.

When the host was assembled, Lugh led them into Connacht and smote the Fomorians and drove them to their ships. But of this the tale tells not here. When the fight was done, Lugh asked of his comrades if they had seen his father in the fight and how it fared with him. They said they had not seen him. Lugh made search among the dead, and they found not Kian there.

"Were Kian alive he would be here," said Lugh. "I swear by the Wind and the Sun that I will not eat or drink till I know what has befallen him."

On their return the Danaan host passed by the Plain of Murthemny, and when they came near the place of the murder the stones cried aloud to Lugh. They told him of the deed of the sons of Turenn. Then Lugh searched for the place of a new grave, and when he had found it he caused it to be dug. The body of his father was raised up, and Lugh saw that it was but a litter of wounds.

He cried out, "Oh, wicked and horrible deed!" He kissed his father. "I am sick from this sight. My eyes are blind from it, my ears are deaf from it, my heart stands still from it. Ye gods that I adore, why was I not here when this crime was done? A man of the children of Dana slain by his fellows."

He lamented long and bitterly. Then Kian was again laid in his grave, and a mound heaped over it and a pillar-stone set thereon. They wrote his name in Ogham, and sung a dirge for him.

After that, Lugh departed to Tara, to the Court of the High King. He charged his people to say nothing of what had happened until he himself had made it known.

When he reached Tara with his victorious host, the King placed Lugh at his own right hand before all the princes and lords of the Danaan folk. Lugh looked round about him, and saw the sons of Turenn sitting among the assembly. They were among the best and strongest and the handsomest of those who were present at that time. None had borne themselves better in the fight with the sea-rovers. Lugh asked of the King that the chain of silence might be shaken. The assembly heard it, and gave their attention to Lugh.

"Oh, King," said Lugh. "And ye princes of the People of Dana, I ask what vengeance would each of you exact upon a man who had foully murdered your father?"

They were all astonished, and the King answered, "Surely it is not the father of Lugh Lamfada who has thus been slain?"

"Thou hast said it," said Lugh, "and those who did the deed are listening to me now, and know it better than I."

The King said, "Not in one day would I slay the murderer of my father, but I would tear from him a limb day by day till he were dead."

So spake all the lords of the Danaans, and the Sons of Turenn among the rest.

"They have sentenced themselves, the murderers of my father," said Lugh. "Nevertheless I shall accept an *eric* from them. If they will pay it, it shall be well. But if not, I shall not break the peace of the King's Assembly and of his sanctuary, but let them beware how they leave the Hall Tara until they have made me satisfaction."

"Had I slain your father," said the High King, "glad should I be to have an *eric* accepted for his blood."

The Sons of Turenn whispered among themselves. "It is to us that Lugh is speaking," said Iuchar and Iucharba. "Let us confess and have the *eric* assessed upon us, for he has knowledge of our deed."

"Nay," said Brian. "He may be seeking for an open confession, and then perchance he would not accept an *eric*."

But the two brethren said to Brian, "Do thou confess because thou art the eldest, or if thou do not, then we shall."

So Brian, son of Turenn, rose up and said to Lugh, "It is to us thou hast spoken, Lugh, since thou knowest there is enmity of old time between our houses. If thou wilt have it that we have slain thy father, and then declare our *eric* and we shall pay it."

"I will take an *eric* from you," said Lugh, "and if it seem too great, I will remit a portion of it."

"Declare it, then," said the Sons of Turenn.

"This it is," said Lugh. "Three apples. The skin of a pig. A spear. Two steeds and a chariot. Seven swine. A whelp of a dog. A cooking spit. Three shouts on a hill."

"We would not consider heavy hundreds or thousands of these things," said the Sons of Turenn, "but we misdoubt thou hast some secret purpose against us."

"I deem it no small *eric*," answered Lugh. "I call to witness the High King and lords of the Danaans that I shall ask no more, and do ye on your side give me guarantees for the fulfilment of it."

So the High King and the lords of the Danaans entered into bonds with Lugh and with the Sons of Turenn: that the *eric* should be paid and would wipe out the blood of Kian.

"Now," said Lugh, "it is better for me to give you fuller knowledge of the *eric*. The three apples that I have demanded of you are the apples that grow in the garden of the Hesperides, in the east of the world, and none but these will do. Thus it is with them: they are the color of bright gold, and as large as the head of a month old child. The taste of them is like honey; if he who eats them has any running sore or evil disease it is healed by them. They may be eaten and eaten and never be less. I doubt, oh young heroes, if ye will get these apples, for those who guard them know well an ancient prophecy that one day three knights from the western world would come to attempt them.

"As for the skin of the pig, that is a treasure of Tuish, the King of Greece. If it be laid upon a wounded man it will make him whole and well, if only it overtake the breath of life in him. And do ye know what is the spear that I demanded?"

"We do not," said they.

"It is the poisoned spear of Peisear, the King of Persia. So fierce is the spirit of war in it that it must be kept in a pot of soporific herbs or it would fly out raging for death. And do ye know what are the two horses and the chariot ye must get?"

"We do not know," said they.

"The steeds and the chariot belong to Dobar, King of Sicily. They are magic steeds and can go indifferently over land and sea. Nor can they be killed by any weapon unless they be torn in pieces and their bones cannot be found. And the seven pigs are the swine of Asal, King of the Golden Pillars, which may be slain and eaten every night and the next morning they are alive again.

"And the hound-whelp I asked of you is the whelp of the King of Iorroway, that can catch and slay any beast in the world. Hard it is to get possession of that whelp.

"The cooking spit is one of the spits that the faery women of the Island of Finchory have in their kitchen.

"And the hill on which ye must give three shouts is the hill where dwells Mochaen in the north of Lochlann. Now Mochaen and his sons have it as a sacred ordinance that they permit not any man to raise a shout upon their hill. With him it was that my father was trained to arms, and if I forgave ye his death, yet would Mochaen not forgive it.

"And now ye know the *eric* which ye have to pay for the slaying of Kian, son of Canta."

Astonishment and despair overcame the Sons of Turenn when they learned the meaning of the *eric* of Lugh, and they went home to tell the tidings to their father.

"This is an evil tale," said Turenn. "I doubt but death and doom shall come from your seeking of that *eric,* and it is but right they should. Yet it may be that ye shall obtain the *eric* if Lugh or Mananan will help you to it. Go now to Lugh, and ask him for the loan of the faery steed of Mananan, which was given him to ride over the sea into Erin. He will refuse you, for he will say that the steed is but lent to him and he may not make a loan of a loan. Then ask him for the loan of Ocean Sweeper, which is the magic boat of Mananan, and that he must give, for it is a sacred ordinance with Lugh not to refuse a second petition."

So they went to Lugh, and it all fell out as Turenn had told them, and they went back to Turenn.

"Ye have done something towards the *eric*," said Turenn, "but not much. Yet Lugh would be well pleased that ye brought him whatever might serve him when the Fomorians come to the battle again, and well pleased would he be that ye might get your death in bringing it. Go now, my sons, and blessing and victory be with you."

The Sons of Turenn went down to the harbor on the Boyne River where the Boat of Mananan was, and Ethne their sister with them.

When they reached the place, Ethne broke into lamentations and weeping, but Brian said, "Weep not, dear sister, but let us go forth gaily to great deeds. Better a hundred deaths in the quest of honor than to live and die as cowards and sluggards."

But Ethne said, "Ye are banished from Erin; never was there a sadder deed."

Then they put forth from the river mouth of the Boyne and soon the fair coasts of Erin faded out of sight. "And now," said they among themselves, "what course shall we steer?"

"No need to steer the Boat of Mananan," said Brian. He whispered to the Boat, "Bear us swiftly, Boat of Mananan, to the Garden of the Hesperides,"

The spirit of the Boat heard him and leaped eagerly forward, lifting and dipping over the rollers and throwing up an arch of spray each side of its bows wherein sat a rainbow when the sun shone upon it. So in no long time they drew nigh to the coast where was the far-famed garden of the Golden Apples.

"And now, how shall we set about the capture of the apples?" asked Brian.

"Draw sword and fight for them," said Iuchar and Iucharba. "If we are the stronger, we shall win them, and if not, we shall fall, as fall we surely must ere the *eric* for Kian be paid."

"Nay," said Brian. "Whether we live or die, let not men say of us that we went blind and headlong to our tasks. But rather that we made the head help the hand, and that we deserved to win even though we lost. Now my counsel is that we approach the garden in the shape of three hawks, strong of wing, and that we hover about until the Wardens of the Tree have spent all their darts and javelins in casting at us. Then let us swoop down suddenly and bear off each of us an apple if we may."

So it was agreed. Brian struck himself and each of the brothers with a druid wand, and they became three beautiful, fierce, and strong-winged hawks. When the Wardens perceived them, they shouted and threw showers of arrows and darts at them. But the hawks evaded all of these until the missiles were spent, and then seized each an apple in his talons. But Brian seized two, for he took one in his beak as well. Then they flew as swiftly as they might to the shore where they had left their boat.

Now the King of that garden had three fair daughters, to whom the apples and the garden were very dear, and he transformed the maidens into three griffins, who pursued the hawks. The griffins threw darts of fire, as it were lightning, at the hawks.

"Brian!" cried Iuchar and his brother. "We are being burnt by these darts! We are lost unless we can escape them."

On this, Brian changed himself and his brethren into three swans. They plunged into the sea and the burning darts were quenched. Then the griffins gave over the chase, and the Sons of Turenn made for their boat, and they embarked with the four apples. Thus their first quest was ended.

After that they resolved to seek the pigskin from the King of Greece, and debated how they should come before him.

"Let us," said Brian, "assume the character and garb of poets and men of learning, for such are wont to come from

Ireland and to travel foreign lands. In that character shall the Greeks receive us best, for such men have honor among them."

"It is well said," replied the brothers. "Yet we have no poems in our heads, and how to compose one we know not."

Howbeit they dressed their hair in the fashion of the poets of Erin, and went up to the palace of Tuish the King. The doorkeeper asked of them who they were, and what was their business.

"We are bards from Ireland," they said. "We have come with a poem to the King."

"Let them be admitted," said the King, when the doorkeeper brought him that tale. "They have doubtless come thus far to seek a powerful patron."

So Brian and Iuchar and Iucharba came in and were made welcome, and were entertained. The minstrels of the King of Greece chanted the lays of that country before them. After that came the turn of the stranger bards, and Brian asked his brethren if they had anything to recite.

"We have not," said they. "We know but one art: to take what we want by the strong hand if we may, and if we may not, to die fighting."

"That is a difficult art too," said Brian. "Let us see how we thrive with the poetry."

So he rose up and recited this lay:

> *"Mighty is thy fame, O King,*
> *Towering like a giant oak;*
> *For my song I ask no thing*
> *Save a pigskin for a cloak.*
>
> *When a neighbor with his friend*
> *Quarrels, they are ear to ear;*

Who on us their store shall spend
Shall be richer than they were.

Armies of the storming wind,
Raging seas, the sword's fell stroke,
Thou hast nothing to my mind
Save thy pigskin for a cloak."

"That is a very good poem," said the King. "But one word of its meaning I do not understand."

"I will interpret it for you," said Brian. *"'Mighty is thy fame, O King, Towering like a giant oak.'*

"That is to say, as the oak surpasses all the other trees of the forest, so do you surpass all the kings of the world in goodness, in nobleness, and in liberality.

"'A pigskin for a cloak.'

"That is the skin of the pig of Tuish, which I would fain receive as the reward for my lay.

"'When a neighbor with his friend Quarrels, they are ear to ear.'

"That is to signify that you and I shall be about each other's ears over the skin, unless you are willing to give it to me. Such is the sense of my poem."

"I would praise your poem more," said the King, "if there were not so much about my pigskin in it. Little sense have you, O man of poetry, to make that request of me, for not to all the poets, scholars, and lords of the world would I give that skin of my own free will. But what I will do is this: I will give the full of that skin of red gold thrice over in reward for your poem."

"Thanks be to you for that," said Brian. "I knew that I asked too much, but I knew also thou wouldst redeem the skin amply and generously. And now let the gold be duly measured out in it, for greedy am I, and I will not abate an ounce of it."

The servants of the King were then sent with Brian and his brothers to the King's treasure chamber to measure out the gold. As they did so, Brian suddenly snatched the skin from the hands of him who held it, and swiftly wrapped it round his body. Then the three brothers drew sword and made for the door, and a great fight arose in the King's palace. But they hewed and thrust manfully on every side of them, and though sorely wounded they fought their way through and escaped to the shore, and drove their boat out to sea where the skin of the magic pig quickly made them whole and sound again. And thus the second quest of the Sons of Turenn had its end.

"Let us now," said Brian, "Go to seek the spear of the King of Persia."

"In what manner of guise shall we go before the King of Persia?" asked his brothers.

"As we did before the King of Greece," said Brian.

"That guise served us well with the King of Greece," replied they. "Nevertheless, oh Brian, this business of professing to be poets, when we are but swordsmen, is painful to us."

However, they dressed their hair in the manner of poets and went up boldly to the palace of King Peisear of Persia, saying, as before, that they were wandering bards from Ireland who had a poem to recite before the King. As they passed through the courtyard they marked the spear drowsing in its pot of sleepy herbs. They were made welcome, and after listening to the lays of the King's minstrel, Brian rose and sang:

> "'Tis little Peisear cares for spears,
> Since armies, when his face they see,
> All overcome with panic fears
> Without a wound they turn and flee.

The Yew is monarch of the wood,
No other tree disputes its claim.
The shining shaft in venom stewed
Flies fiercely forth to kill and maim.'

"Tis a very good poem," said the King. "But, oh bard from Erin, I do not understand your reference to my spear."

"It is merely this," replied Brian. "That I would like your spear as a reward for my poem."

The King stared at Brian, and his beard bristled with anger. "Never was a greater reward paid for any poem than not to adjudge you guilty of instant death for your request."

Brian flung at the king the fourth golden apple that he had taken from the Garden of the Hesperides, and it dashed out his brains. Immediately the brothers all drew sword and made for the courtyard. Here they seized the magic spear, and with it and with their swords they fought their way clear, not without many wounds, and escaped to their boat. And thus ended the third quest of the Sons of Turenn.

Now having come safely and victoriously through so many straits and perils, they began to be merry and hoped that all the *eric* might yet be paid. So they sailed away with high hearts to the Island of Sicily, to get the two horses and the chariot of the King. The Boat of Mananan bore them swiftly and well.

Having arrived here, they debated among themselves as to how they should proceed. They agreed to present themselves as Irish mercenary soldiers; for such were wont in those days to take service with foreign kings. Until they should learn where the horses and the chariot were kept, and how they should come at them. They went forward, and found the King and his lords in the palace garden taking the air.

The Sons of Turenn then paid homage to him, and he asked them of their business.

"We are Irish mercenary soldiers," they said, "seeking our wages from the kings of the world."

"Are ye willing to take service with me?" said the King.

"We are," said they, "and to that end are we come."

Their contract of military service was made. They remained at the King's court for a month and a fortnight, and did not in all that time come to see the steeds or the chariot.

At last Brian said, "Things are going ill with us, my brethren, in that we know no more at this day of the steeds or of the chariot than when we first arrived at this place."

"What shall we do, then?" asked they.

"Let us do this. Let us gird on our arms and all our marching array, and tell the King that we shall quit his service unless he show us the chariot."

And so they did, and the King said, "Tomorrow shall be a gathering and parade of all my host. The chariot shall be there, and ye shall see it if ye have a mind."

So the next day the steeds were yoked and the chariot was driven round a great plain before the King and his lords. Now these steeds could run as well on sea as on dry land, and they were swifter than the winds of March. As the chariot came round the second time, Brian's brothers seized the horses' heads, and Brian took the charioteer by the foot and flung him out over the rail. They all leaped into the chariot and drove away. Such was the swiftness of their driving that they were out of sight ere the King and his men knew rightly what had befallen. And thus ended the fourth quest of the Sons of Turenn.

Next they betook themselves to the court of Asal, King of the Golden Pillars, to get the seven swine which might be eaten every night, but would be whole and well on the morrow morn.

It had now been noised about every country that three young heroes from Erin were plundering the kings of the world of their treasures in payment of a mighty *eric*. When they arrived at the Land of the Golden Pillars they found the harbor guarded and a watch kept, that no one who might resemble the Sons of Turenn should enter.

But Asal the King came to the harbor mouth and spoke with the heroes, for he was desirous to see those who had done the great deeds that he had heard of. He asked them if it were true that they had done such things, and why. Brian told him the story of the mighty *eric* which had been laid upon them, and what they had done and suffered in fulfilling it.

"Why," said King Asal, "have ye now come to my country?"

"For the seven swine. To take them with us as a part of that *eric*."

"How do you mean to get them?" asked the King.

"With your goodwill," replied Brian. "If so it may be, and to pay you therefore with all the wealth we now have, which is thanks and love, and to stand by your side hereafter in any strait or quarrel you may enter into. But if you will not grant us the swine, and we may not be quit of our *eric* without them, we shall even take them as we may, and as we have beforetime taken mighty treasures from mighty kings."

King Asal went into counsel with his lords, and he advised that the swine be given to the Sons of Turenn. Partly for that he was moved with their desperate plight and the hardihood they had shown, and partly that they might get them whether or no. To this they all agreed, and the Sons of Turenn were invited to come ashore, where they were courteously and hospitably entertained in the King's palace.

On the morrow the pigs were given to them, and great was their gladness, for never before had they won a treasure without toil and blood. They vowed that, if they should live, the name of Asal should be made by them a great and shining name, for the compassion and generosity he had shown them. This, then, was the fifth quest of the Sons of Turenn.

"And whither do ye voyage now?" said Asal to them.

"We go," replied they, "to Iorroway for the hound's whelp which is there."

"Take me with you, then. For the King of Iorroway is husband to my daughter, and I may prevail upon him to grant you the hound without combat."

So the King's ship was manned and provisioned, and the Sons of Turenn laid up their treasures in the Boat of Mananan, and they all sailed joyfully forth to the pleasant kingdom of Iorroway. But here, too, they found all the coasts and harbors guarded, and entrance was forbidden them.

Asal declared who he was, and him they allowed to land. He journeyed to where his son-in-law, the King of Iorroway, was. To him Asal related the whole story of the sons of Turenn, and why they were come to that kingdom.

"Thou wert a fool," said the King of Iorroway, "to have come on such a mission. There are no three heroes in the world to whom the Immortals have granted such grace that they should get my hound either by favor or by fight."

"That is not a good word," said Asal. "For the treasures they now possess have made them yet stronger than they were, and these they won in the teeth of kings as strong as thou."

And much more he said to him to persuade him to yield up the hound, but in vain. So Asal took his way back to the haven where the Sons of Turenn lay, and told them his tidings. Then the Sons of Turenn seized the magic spear, and the pigskin, and with a rush like that of three eagles descending from a high cliff upon a lamb-fold they burst upon the guards of the King of Iorroway. Fierce and fell was the combat that ensued, and many times the brothers were driven apart, and all but overborne by the throng of their foes. But at last Brian perceived where the King of Iorroway was directing the fight, and he cut his way to him. Having smitten him to the ground, he bound him and carried him out of the press to the haven-side where Asal was.

"There," he said, "is your son-in-law for you Asal, and I swear by my sword that I had more easily killed him thrice than once to bring him thus bound to you."

"That is very like," said Asal. "But now hold him to ransom."

The people of Iorroway gave the hound to the Sons of Turenn as a ransom for their King. The King was released, and friendship and alliance were made between them. With joyful hearts the Sons of Turenn bade farewell to the King of Iorroway and to Asal, and departed on their way. Thus was the sixth of their quests fulfilled.

Now Lugh Lamfada desired to know how the Sons of Turenn had fared, and whether they had got any portion of the great *eric* that might be serviceable to him when the Fomorians should return for one more struggle. And by sorcery and divination it was revealed to him how they had thriven, and that nought remained to be won save the

cooking-spit of the sea-nymphs, and to give the three
shouts upon the hill.

Lugh then by druidic art caused a spell of oblivion and
forgetfulness to descend upon the Sons of Turenn, and put
into their hearts withal a yearning and passion to return to
their native land of Erin. They forgot, therefore, that a
portion of the *eric* was still to win, and they bade the Boat
of Mananan bear them home with their treasures. They
deemed that they should now quit them of all their debt for
the blood of Kian and live free in their father's home,
having done such things and won such fame as no three
brothers had ever done since the world began.

At the Brugh of Boyne, where they had started on their
quest, their boat came ashore again. As they landed they
wept for joy, and falling on their knees they kissed the
green sod of Erin. Then they took up their treasures and
journeyed to Ben Edar, where the High King of Ireland,
and Lugh with him, were holding an Assembly of the
People of Dana. When Lugh heard that they were on their
way he put on his cloak of invisibility and withdrew privily
to Tara.

When the brethren arrived at Ben Edar, the High King
of the lords of the Danaans gave them welcome and
applause. All were rejoiced that the stain of ancient feud
and bloodshed should be wiped out, and that the Children
of Dana should be at peace within their borders. Then they
sought for Lugh to deliver over the *eric*, but he was not to
be found.

Brian said, "He has gone to Tara to avoid us, having
heard that we were coming with our treasures and weapons
of war."

Word was then sent to Lugh at Tara that the Sons of
Turenn were at Ben Edar, and the *eric* with them.

"Let them pay it over to the High King," said Lugh.

So it was done. When Lugh had tidings that the High
King had the *eric*, he returned to Ben Edar where the *eric*
was laid before him.

"Is the debt paid, oh Lugh, son of Kian?" asked Brian.

Lugh said, "Truly there is here the price of any man's
death. But it is not lawful to give a quittance for an *eric* that
is not complete. Where is the cooking-spit from the Island
of Finchory? And have ye given the three shouts upon the
Hill of Mochaen?"

At this word Brian and Iuchar and Iucharba fell prone
upon the ground, speechless awhile from grief and dismay.
After a time they left the Assembly like broken men, with
hanging heads and heavy steps. They betook themselves to
Dún Turenn, where they found their father, and they told
him all that had befallen them since they had parted with
him and set forth on the Quest. Thus they passed the night
in gloom and evil forebodings, and on the morrow they
went down once more to the place where the Boat of
Mananan was moored.

Again, Ethne their sister accompanied them, wailing
and lamenting, but no words of cheer had they now to say
to her. For now they began to comprehend that a mightier
and a craftier mind had caught them in the net of fate. And
whereas they had deemed themselves heroes and victors in
the most glorious quest whereof the earth had record, they
now knew that they were but as arrows in the hands of a
laughing archer, who shoots one at a stag and one at the
heart of a foe, and one, it may be, in sheer wantonness, and
to try his bow, over a cliff edge into the sea.

However, they put forth in their magic boat, but in no
wise could they direct it to the Isle of Finchory, and a
quarter of a year they traversed the seaways and never
could get tidings of that island. At last Brian fashioned for
himself by magic art a water-dress, with a helmet of crystal,

and into the depths of the sea he plunged. Here, the story tells, he searched hither and thither for a fortnight, till at last he found that island, which was an island indeed with the sea over it and around it and beneath it. There dwelt the red-haired ocean-nymphs in glittering palaces among the sea-flowers, and they wrought fair embroidery with gold and jewels, and sang, as they wrought, a faery music like the chiming of silver bells. Three fifties of them sat or played in their great hall as Brian entered, and they gazed on him but spoke no word. Then Brian strode to the wide hearth, and without a word he seized from it a spit that was made of beaten gold, and turned again to go.

But at that the laughter of the sea-maidens rippled through the hall and one of them said, "Thou art a bold man, Brian, and bolder than thou knowest. For if thy two brothers were here, the weakest of us could vanquish all the three. Nevertheless, take the spit for thy daring; we had never granted it for thy prayers."

Brian thanked them and bade farewell, and he rose to the surface of the water. Ere long his brethren perceived him as he shouldered the waves on the bosom of the deep, and they sailed to where he was and took him on board. And thus ended the quest for the seventh portion of the *eric* of Kian.

After that their hopes revived a little, and they set sail for the land of Lochlann, in which was the Hill of Mochaen. When they had arrived at the hill, Mochaen came out to meet them with his three sons, Corc and Conn and Hugh. Never did the Sons of Turenn ever behold a band of grimmer and mightier warriors than those four.

"What seek ye here?" demanded Mochaen of them.

They told him that it had been laid upon them to give three shouts upon the hill.

"It hath been laid upon me," said Mochaen, "to prevent this thing."

Brian and Mochaen drew sword and fell furiously upon each other. Their fighting was like that of two hungry lions or two wild bulls, until at last Brian drove his sword into the throat of Mochaen, and he died.

With that the Sons of Mochaen and the Sons of Turenn rushed fiercely upon each other. Long and sore was the strife that they had, and the blood that fell made red the grassy place wherein they fought. Not one of them but received wounds that pierced him through and through, and that heroes of less hardihood had died of a score of times. But in the end the sons of Mochaen fell, and Brian, Iuchar, and Iucharba lay over them in a swoon-like death.

After a while Brian's senses came back to him. "Do ye live, dear brothers, or how is it with you?"

"We are as good as dead," said they. "Let us be."

"Arise," ordered Brian. "For truly I feel death coming swiftly upon us, and we have yet to give the three shouts upon the hill."

"We cannot stir," said Iuchar and Iucharba.

Brian rose to his knees and to his feet, and he lifted up his two brothers while the blood of all three streamed down to their feet. They raised their voices as best they might, and gave three hoarse cries upon the Hill of Mochaen. And thus was the last of the epic fulfilled.

They bound up their wounds, and Brian placed himself between the two brothers, and slowly and painfully they made their way to the boat, and put out to sea for Ireland.

As they lay in the stupor of faintness in the boat, one murmured to himself, "I see the Cape of Ben Edar and the coast of Turenn, and Tara of the Kings."

Then Iuchar and Iucharba entreated Brian to lift their heads upon his breast. "Let us but see the land of Erin again," begged they. "The hills around Tailtin, and the dewy plain of Bregia, and the quiet waters of the Boyne and our father's *Dún* thereby. Healing will come to us, or if death come we can endure it after that."

Brian raised them up and they saw that they were now nearby under Ben Edar, and at the Strand of the Bull they took land. They were then conveyed to the *Dún* of Turenn, and life was still in them when they were laid in their father's hall.

And Brian said to Turenn, "Go now, dear father, with all speed to Lugh at Tara. Give him the cooking-spit, and tell how thou hast found us after giving our three shouts upon the Hill of Mochaen. Then beseech him that he yield thee the loan of the pigskin of the King of Greece, for if it be laid upon us while the life is yet in us, we shall recover. We have won the *eric*, and it may be that he will not pursue us to our death."

Turenn went to Lugh and gave him the spit of the sea-nymphs, and besought him for the lives of his sons.

Lugh was silent for a while, but his countenance did not change. "Thou, old man, seest nought but the cloud of sorrow wherein thou art encompassed. But I hear from above it the singing of the Immortal Ones, who tell to one another the story of this land. Thy sons must die; yet have I shown to them more mercy than they showed to Kian. I have forgiven them, but they shall not live to slay their own immortality. The royal bards of Erin and the old men in the chimney corners shall tell of their glory and their fate as long as the land shall endure."

Turenn bowed his white head and went sorrowfully back to *Dún* Turenn. He told his sons of the words that Lugh had said. With that the sons of Turenn kissed each other, and the breath of life departed from them, and they died.

And Turenn died also, for his heart was broken in him, and Ethne his daughter buried them in one grave. Thus, then, ends the tale of the Quest of the *Eric* and the Fate of the Sons of Turenn.

Glossary

bar an suan	a pin of slumber
bason	basin
birdeen	young bird or girl
bodach	old man
bohalawn	rag-weed
bothy	shelter
carcase	carcass
cartron	quarter of land
cronan	purr
cronawn	hum
curragh	boat
Diachbha	the fates
Dún	fort
eric	fine
erinach	Irish man
kŭ́ran	small vessel
liefer	readily
Musha	term of affection
omadawn	simpleton
rath	circular enclosure
rookawn	row, noise
sheehogues	faery people
slat an draoichta	rod of enchantment
soorawn	causing dizziness
toirm	uproar
traneens	blades of grass
tympan	instrument
wether	castrated ram
wight	human being

A bestselling author and editor, Lizzy's published works span many genres, including thriller, science fiction, Celtic nonfiction, fantasy, stage and screenplays.

Lizzy's career is as varied as the genres she writes. Starting out as a library assistant in a Northern Irish rural town, she moved on to study Theatre Arts and Literature in London, and toured the United Kingdom as a professional actress. Roles ranged from the goddess Hecate in Shakespeare's Macbeth to Gustav, the Amazing Dancing Bear in a clown troupe.

Her writing career began after she immigrated to the United States and adapted a stage play version of LM Montgomery's Anne of Gables for the Oregon Children's Theatre Company, which toured nationally.

www.lizzyshannon.com

Slidderyford Dolmen, County Down

A SONG OF BULLETS by Belfast born Lizzy Shannon, who grew up during the worst of 'The Troubles' of the 80s. A terrorist bomb sets off a chain reaction in musician Jennifer Hamilton's life, causing destruction, betrayal, and vengeance. She enters the traditional Belfast music scene to infiltrate the IRA, also entering a dangerous love triangle. A unique point of view, based on a true story. Recruited by one side to spy on the other, which will she ultimately choose?

"Entertaining and artfully done. Everything you ever wanted to know about our deeply flawed country.
-- Gerry Anderson, Radio Ulster

"Shannon is clearly drawing on her own personal background and experiences as a Northern Irish native ...
enriched by historical references...a touch of romance that should impress readers with its political acumen."

In this beautiful larger journal edition of A CELTIC YEARBOOK, Lizzy Shannon takes us through the Gregorian calendar as well as the 13 months and single day of the Druidic calendar. Included new tidbits of Celtic and Druidic lore! Like the Native Americans, Celtic traditions were handed down through the generations. Explore legends and superstitions, find out how to make honey mead, hand-made soap, and learn about the Celtic astrological signs that are based on the Dryadic personalities of individual trees. Discover which sign you were born under, who your Celtic spirit animal guide is, and much more.

"The spirit of Ireland shared in a delightfully personal and entertaining little book." - *Gerry Anderson, Radio Foyle Northern Ireland, author of Surviving Stroke City and Heads.*

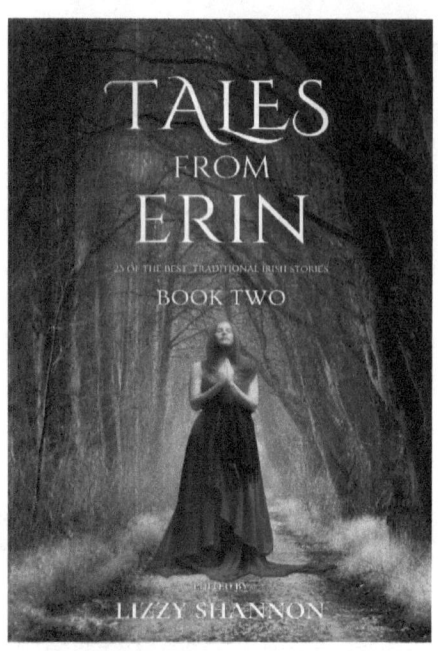

MORE TALES FROM ERIN – AN ANTHOLOGY OF STORIES is a rich and captivating collection that breathes new life into the myth, mystery, and folklore of Ireland. From the emerald hills and ancient stone circles to windswept coasts and hidden glens, this anthology gathers voices—both old and imagined—to weave together a tapestry of tales as timeless as the land itself.

Within these pages, readers will encounter brave warriors, mischievous fairies, tragic heroes, wise women, and restless spirits. Some stories echo the legendary sagas of old; others are fresh interpretations or original tales inspired by the deep cultural wellspring of Erin. Together, they explore themes of love, loss, magic, rebellion, and belonging—all rooted in the soul of Ireland.

Whether revisiting familiar legends or discovering new fables, More Tales from Erin invites you on a journey across ages and imaginations. It is a tribute to the enduring power of storytelling, and a celebration of Ireland's spirit—wild, lyrical, and alive with wonder.

The Time Twist Series: In 2019, Catriona Logan is just an ordinary young woman—until a temporal experiment from the future goes disastrously wrong and throws her into a time that barely resembles Earth. The planet is now a scorched wasteland, and what's left of humanity serves the feline-like Leontors in a brutal war against the reptilian Dracans.

Victory is out of reach—until Catriona arrives. Her 21st-century brainwaves are a priceless anomaly, capable of shifting the tide of battle. Both alien factions want her. Whoever scans her mind first will win the war—and control the future of Earth.

Hunted, captured, and caught in a tangled web of lies, Catriona must navigate a world where nothing is familiar, trust is a luxury, and time is dangerously broken. Her only hope may lie in an unlikely ally... and in finding the strength to rewrite the rules of a game she never chose to play.

"A fast-paced romp through an imaginative wild world inhabited with memorable characters and a fearless, fiery heroine. Strap yourself in for a thrilling trip." – *Ray Pitz, Editor, Pamplin Media Group*

Sheffield Publications

www.ingramcontent.com/pod-product-compliance
Lightning Source LLC
Chambersburg PA
CBHW031309120626
46554CB00001BA/350